Collins gem

Sharks

Leonard Compagno
Marc Dando
Sarah Fowler

Collins

An Imprint of HarperCollins*Publisher.*

ISBN-10: 0-00-721986-5
ISBN-13: 978-0-00-721986-5

ISBN-10: 0-06-084976-2 (in the United States)
ISBN-13: 978-0-06-084976-4
FIRST U.S. EDITION Published 2006

HarperCollins books may be purchased for educational, business, or
sales promotional use. For information in the United States, please
write to: Special Markets Department, HarperCollins Publishers, 10 East
53rd Street, New York, NY 10022.

Text © 2006 Sarah Fowler and Leonard Compagno
Artwork © Fluke Art
Illustrations © Marc Dando

Printed and bound in Italy by Amadeus S.p.A.

10 09 08 07 06
9 8 7 6 5 4 3 2 1

CONTENTS

WHAT IS A SHARK?

Taoxonomy is science of classifying living things. It started in the late sixteenth century when people first became concerned with finding a way of arranging minerals, plants, and animals into groupings, which they called *methodus*, or method. One of the most prominent taxonomists was the Swedish botanist Carolus Linnaeus (1707–1778). His groups have since been revised a little but it is still the Linnaen system that is used to classify living organisms today.

The system is made up of a series of groups, starting with the highest (and largest) category, the kingdom. Sharks form part of the animal kingdom. Below the kingdom is the phylum, which includes all vertebrate animals in the phylum chordata. This is followed by the class, and all sharks belong to the class Chondrichthyes. The next group is the order, for example, Elasmobranchii, which includes all of the closely related sharks, skates, and rays. Then comes the family, i.e. Lamnidae (Mackerel Sharks), followed by the genus, for example, Carcharodon, which is derived from the Greek "to sharpen" and "teeth"—and then the species.

All sharks belong to the taxonomic class Chondrichthyes, or cartilaginous fish. All of the fish in this class have a simple internal skeleton formed from flexible cartilage. There is no true bone present in their skeleton, fins, or scales. All have gill slits on the sides of their heads and their pectoral fins are not attached to the head above the gill openings. They also have a large caudal fin (tail) and one or two dorsal fins (sometimes with spines).

The sharks are not the only cartilaginous fishes, or Chondrichthyes. Scientists classify all of the closely related sharks, skates, and rays as Elasmobranchii ("elasmo" means plate and "branchii" means gills). Elasmobranchs have five to seven pairs of gill openings on the sides of their head.

The main difference between sharks and the skates and rays (or batoid fishes, not included in this book) is that rays have large flat pectoral fins attached to the sides of their heads above the gill openings and usually a short, flat body. That's why they are sometimes known affectionately as "pancake sharks." There are more than 600 species of rays.

The chimaeras, or Holocephali, are more distant relatives of sharks. Their four pairs of gill openings are covered and protected by a soft gill cover with one opening on each side of the head. The chimaeras are a very ancient group of cartilaginous fishes, mostly extinct; only about 40 species survive today.

All of the Chondrichthyes also have an upper and lower jaw and nostrils below their head. This distinguishes them from the really primitive fishes, such as the jawless lampreys and hagfish, which also have a cartilaginous skeleton. The Chondrichthyes and the bony fishes (or teleosts) evolved from similar primitive ancestors around 400 million years ago.

INSIDE A SHARK

The cartilaginous skeleton makes sharks incredibly supple and flexible, while an upper jaw without a rigid attachment to the skull makes it easy for them to take huge bites from their prey. The stiff collagenous fibers that support shark fins provide the key ingredient to shark fin soup. Shark teeth, which grow in multiple horizontal rows along the edges of the jaws, continually move forward to replace old teeth that become worn and fall out in huge numbers, often ending up

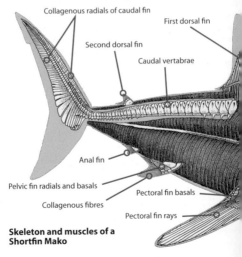

Collagenous radials of caudal fin

First dorsal fin

Second dorsal fin

Caudal vertabrae

Anal fin

Pelvic fin radials and basals

Collagenous fibres

Pectoral fin basals

Pectoral fin rays

Skeleton and muscles of a Shortfin Mako

as fossils. Sharks are typically protected by a very tough skin, usually covered with small, sharp toothlike scales, also known as dermal denticles.

Active sharks have large hearts that pump a lot of blood from the gills (where oxygen is obtained from seawater) to the muscles. Swimming hard creates heat; some sharks can control this heat and are warm-blooded like mammals, which makes them more efficient predators and faster growing than cold-blooded shark species.

The liver fills most of the shark's body cavity—sometimes making up 25% of the body weight. It contains oils that provide buoyancy (sharks have no swim bladder) and stores energy. The "J" shaped stomach is used for food storage and some digestion. Some sharks can cough up their stomachs to empty them. The short intestine contains a spiral valve with a very large surface area for digestion of food. Waste products then pass into the cloaca and vent.

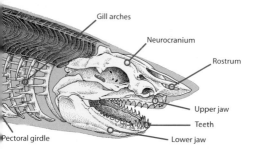

Gill arches

Neurocranium

Rostrum

Upper jaw

Teeth

Pectoral girdle

Lower jaw

SENSES

Shark senses are vital for survival. Smell and taste are of huge importance—not only for detecting prey or other food items at long distance, but also for detecting other shark pheromones, in order to find mates. Sharks might even rely on these senses to help with navigation during their long transoceanic journeys to find feeding, mating, and pupping grounds.

There is a complex system of nasal flaps in front of the mouth that direct incoming water over membranes so sensitive that even the tiniest scent can be picked up. The shark then closes in on the source by swimming up a current and constantly changing direction to ensure that the signal in each nostril is as strong in the other.

Vision is also very important, taking over from taste and smell once the shark is closer to the target. In top predators such as the White Shark, the eyes are very sophisticated and similar to those of mammals. The iris surrounds a pupil that can be opened wide to let in a lot of light or contracted to a pinhole. Like cats' eyes, sharks' eyes allow light to "bounce around" inside the eye to improve vision in very low levels of light (this is what is happening when a cat's eyes seem to glow in the dark). Sharks that are active in shallow water can actually release a layer of pigment (color, or dye) to cover this effect during the day. Deepwater and nocturnal sharks are remarkable for their huge glowing eyes, which are designed to capture as much light as possible in the darkness of the deep ocean. Sharks cannot close their eyelids to protect their eyes, but some groups have developed a third eyelid called the nictitating lower eyelid in order to do this.

Another shark sense that is similar to those of mammals is the detection of changes in pressure. Sound is simply changes in pressure causing vibrations in air or water that are picked up by the inner ear, and although sharks don't have outer ears, their inner ears are incredibly sensitive. Touch is the detection of changes in pressure applied to the skin, but sharks also have a very clever system that no other animal has, and this system operates the lateral line. This lateral line runs along each side of the body of the shark, with additional rows of sense organs around the head and mouth, and sometimes scattered elsewhere along the body. When the water pressure changes, even slightly, it causes tiny "hairs" (neuromasts) inside the shark to move and send nerve pulses to the brain. The brain then interprets these signals and can identify the pressure changes as prey, predator, or another shark.

Sharks are also expert at detecting the minute electric fields given off by animals, inanimate objects, and water moving through the earth's magnetic field. This enables them to sense prey at very close range, even when it's buried deep in the seabed.

Sensory nerve

Sensory cells embedded in a jellylike dome

Canal running length of lateral line system

Skin layers

Tube from canal to outside water

Dermal denticles

Cross section of the lateral line system

HOW A SHARK SWIMS

To swim, sharks shorten the long muscle fibers that run from their head to tail, first on one side of the body, then on the other. This pulls the central vertebral column (or spine) into a series of waves, as shown below. This movement produces forward thrust and acceleration, while the caudal fin (tail) powers the forward movement as it sweeps from side to side.

Sharks need more than just muscles and a tail to swim. Other fins are also vitally important. The large paired pectoral fins act somewhat like wings to counteract the downward movement also produced by the sweeping tail. Dorsal fins help keep the body upright, while the fastest oceanic swimmers also have two broad keels in front of the tail to provide extra stability.

The fastest and most efficient swimmers, including Mako Sharks, have crescent-shaped tails and chunky teardrop-shaped bodies that do not bend much. They use very little energy when cruising.

Swimming sequence of a catshark

In contrast, inefficient swimmers like the primitive frilled and cow sharks have long thin bodies with long upper tail lobes (bottom right) and swim with a very sinuous movement that wastes a lot of energy. The very long upper tail lobe of thresher sharks (center) seems to be an adaptation for herding, striking, and stunning their prey, rather than for faster movement.

Quite a few poor swimmers, including some bullhead sharks, probably spend as much time using their well-muscled mobile paired fins to walk around on the seabed as they do swimming. The Epaulette Shark can even scuttle around out of the water between rock pools.

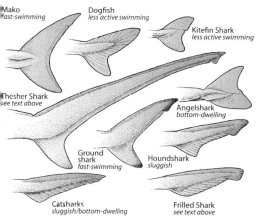

Mako
fast-swimming

Dogfish
less active swimming

Kitefin Shark
less active swimming

Thesher Shark
see text above

Angelshark
bottom-dwelling

Ground shark
fast-swimming

Houndshark
sluggish

Catsharks
sluggish/bottom-dwelling

Frilled Shark
see text above

A variety of tail shapes in nine sharks

HOW SHARKS FEED

Some sharks (for example, Tiger Sharks) will eat almost anything that will fit into their mouths, including tin cans and car license plates. Others take a wide range of prey. In contrast, many are "picky" about their food and are specialized to feed on a relatively small range of prey items, although some may switch as they grow larger and the shape of their teeth changes. None are vegetarian.

The huge plankton feeders (Whale, Basking, and Megamouth Sharks) sieve out and trap plankton and small fish in their filamentous gill rakers and have tiny teeth. Whale Sharks are suction feeders. Basking Sharks are ram-feeders, swimming

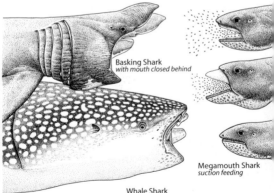

Basking Shark
with mouth closed behind

Megamouth Shark
suction feeding

Whale Shark
with mouth closed behind

steadily, huge mouth wide open, through plankton blooms. Suction-feeding Megamouth Sharks may attract deep ocean prey with luminescent tissue in their mouth.

Many sharks swallow their food whole, catching slippery fish and squids with needlelike backward-pointing teeth. Angel Sharks and Wobbegongs lie in wait on the seabed to suck in passing prey. Shellfish-eaters grind up their food with huge flat teeth. Large predators swallow prey whole or take huge bites out of large animals, protruding their flexible jaws away from the head and rolling back their eyes to protect them from damage in case the meal fights back. Some hunt in packs, dismembering prey much larger than themselves.

Cookiecutter Sharks may use light organs to attract their prey (much larger pelagic fish and marine mammals), latch on, use their thick lips to seal off the area being bitten, and then twist their bodies in order to cut out a neat, circular plug of flesh with their huge, sawlike cutting teeth. They have even taken bites out of the rubber covers on submarine hydrophones!

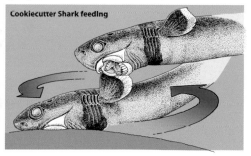

Cookiecutter Shark feeding

FROM EGG TO ADULT

Reproduction takes many forms in sharks, but all require internal fertilization, usually following a period of courtship to ensure the cooperation of females. Mating has only been observed in a few species. In larger sharks, it involves the male biting the female to hold her alongside while using one or two of its paired claspers (grooved extensions of the pelvic fins) to insert packages of sperm into the female reproductive tract. Smaller species twine around each other.

About 40% of sharks are oviparous, which means they lay their eggs onto the seabed. These egg cases have tough coverings and are safely anchored on the seabed with long tendrils that can be wound around seaweed or sea fans. Some are shaped so they can be wedged between rocks or into the mud or sand. The eggs may be laid (often in pairs) at daily or weekly intervals almost immediately after fertilization and depositing the protective egg capsule. The mother often leaves her eggs in nursery grounds, where they can develop safely until the yolk has been absorbed and the young hatch as miniature copies of the adults. The longer the eggs are retained inside the mother, the safer they are. Some spend more than a year on the seabed, while others are laid and hatch within a few weeks. In about 25% of species, the eggs remain inside the mother until after the hatching and she gives birth to fully developed young. These sharks are known as ovoviviparous.

Instead of nourishing their young with a single yolk sac, many species have developed ways to increase the amount of food available to the young inside the female, so that they are larger and better developed at birth and more likely to survive the first dangerous weeks of life in the ocean. Most produce huge numbers of infertile eggs that their growing young find and eat inside the uterus. The Sandtiger Shark pups also eat their weaker brothers and sisters; only one pup survives from each uterus.

About 10% of sharks, including Hammerheads and Blue Sharks, are viviparous, and reproduce in a very similar way to mammals, using a placenta. The yolk sac develops into a placenta and the yolk stalk into a placental cord that transfers nutrients from mother to pup. These sharks can have large litters, but no species of shark provides parental care after birth.

Because sharks usually have to be large in order to produce large pups, most cannot start breeding until they are quite old, and they don't breed every year. Sharks are, therefore, long-lived, slow-growing animals that produce only a relatively small number of pups during their lifetime, but these pups have a good chance of survival. This is fine for large animals at the top of the marine food chain with few natural predators, but it also means that many sharks cannot produce enough young to replace those that are now being killed by man. In contrast, most bony fish produce millions of small eggs, the majority of which will only mature if the species numbers are reduced by fishing, which means that more young can survive to replenish the fishery stocks.

Egg case from an oviparous shark

SHARKS AND PEOPLE

We all need sharks in our oceans. We need them to keep the marine ecosystem in balance and for food (particularly in countries where protein is scarce). We need them for exciting diving and angling adventures, and for the simple joy of knowing that they are somewhere out there—the coolest animals in the world. If we are to keep them, we also need to understand them better.

Truth about sharks can be harder to find than fabulous legends and fiction. The widespread modern view of ferocious man-hunting sharks, like Jaws, differs considerably from the understanding of those living closely with the sea. Many Pacific and Indian Ocean islanders and coastal fishing communities thought that sharks had supernatural powers and protected fisherman. Shark worship, occasionally including human sacrifice, was once fairly common. Some tribes claim sharks as ancestors, and shark calling is still practiced by some Pacific Islanders. Sharks are also important in culture and folklore in Melanesia, West Africa, Australasia, and the Amazon basin. The remains of many large sharks beneath the ruined Aztec Great Temple in Mexico may have been sacrifices to placate bloodthirsty gods.

Sadly, modern stories of shark attacks have now reached even the most remote coastal fishing communities and caused a fear of sharks that contradicts centuries of experience at sea. Worldwide, some 75 to 100 shark attacks are recorded annually, resulting in a few fatalities among the hundreds of millions of individuals who go into the sea for fun or work. The fear of shark attacks is out of all proportion to this tiny risk, although of course the shock and horror that they trigger is understandable. Serious shark attacks are tragedies—partly because they are so rare they are also extremely bad luck.

Most shark attacks are a mistake—a small shark identifies a noise, vibration, or movement as food, takes one bite at the pale flashing hand or foot of a swimmer, and flees immediately it realizes its mistake. The bite is usually so small that no medical treatment is needed. Other "hit and run" attacks occur when large sharks bump and bite the victim, or carry out a sneak attack "out of nowhere" with a single bite. A serious bite from a large shark requires immediate medical attention. Fortunately, most people receive the help they need for survival. Multiple bites and sharks eating human prey are extremely rare.

Shark attacks can occur anywhere that sharks and people may meet in the water and in almost any water depth. They are more likely to occur when very large numbers of people and sharks use the same area, and the number of attacks increases where there are water sports.

**A finned
Whitetip Reef Shark
left to die on the seabed**

Most shark bites take place near dawn or dusk, when sharks tend to hunt. Many occur in murky water, near river mouths, after high rainfall or during onshore winds. The reason for this is probably because these conditions mean it is more likely for the shark to mistake the identity of its prey, and also the murky water means it has approached the prey unnoticed.

Risk of attack is also increased by: thrashing around in the water; swimming with dolphins (they are often accompanied by sharks); swimming alone; urinating in the water; feeding sharks; spearfishing; swimming near boats that are throwing out waste; or wearing strongly contrasting clothing. Really good ways to get bitten include swimming right up to sharks; following them around closely; picking them up; and pulling their tails. Avoid this behavior and treat sharks with the same respect as you would any other large predator with sharp teeth, and the remote chance of your being involved in a shark attack will fall even further.

Sharks are top marine predators that have adapted over hundreds of millions of years to be at the top of the marine food web. They have few natural enemies and only produce a small number of young to replace adults that die from natural causes. Another threat to shark populations is the number of unregulated and encouraged diving encounters for humans. While it is a lucrative industry, there are serious concerns over its impact on shark behavior, habitats, and ecology. Proper, responsibly managed shark encounters can benefit both the shark and the diver, and ensuring that you go with a licensed operator will help secure the future of many shark species and ensure there is no damage to their environment.

**Properly managed shark encounters could
help secure the future of many shark species**

Unfortunately for sharks, increasing fishing effort and technology is now removing them faster than they can breed. Shark fin is one of the most valuable seafood products in the world, and used to be so rare and precious that it was only eaten at the banquets of Chinese emperors. Many other shark products, however, are of low value, but demand is increasing and, with most shark fisheries unmanaged, stocks are rapidly declining. Other major threats to sharks include habitat alteration, damage and loss from coastal developments, pollution, and the impacts of fisheries on the seabed and food species.

TOPOGRAPHY

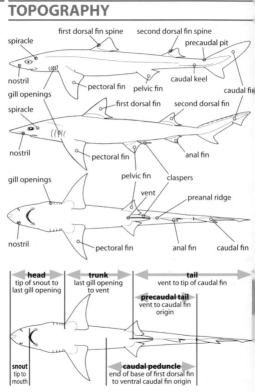

spiracle

first dorsal fin spine   second dorsal fin spine

precaudal pit

nostril

gill openings

pectoral fin   pelvic fin

caudal keel

caudal fin

spiracle

first dorsal fin   second dorsal fin

nostril

pectoral fin

anal fin

gill openings

pelvic fin   claspers

vent

preanal ridge

nostril

pectoral fin   anal fin   caudal fin

head
tip of snout to
last gill opening

trunk
last gill opening
to vent

tail
vent to tip of caudal fin

precaudal tail
vent to caudal fin
origin

snout
tip to
mouth

caudal peduncle
end of base of first dorsal fin
to ventral caudal fin origin

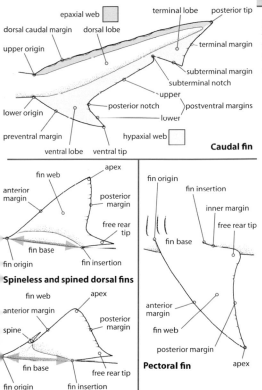

epaxial web

terminal lobe   posterior tip

dorsal caudal margin   dorsal lobe

upper origin

terminal margin

subterminal margin

subterminal notch

upper

posterior notch   postventral margins

lower origin

lower

preventral margin   hypaxial web

ventral lobe   ventral tip

Caudal fin

fin web   apex

anterior margin

posterior margin

free rear tip

fin base

fin origin   fin insertion

Spineless and spined dorsal fins

fin web   apex

anterior margin

spine   posterior margin

fin base

free rear tip

fin origin   fin insertion

fin origin   fin insertion

inner margin

free rear tip

fin base

anterior margin

fin web

posterior margin

Pectoral fin   apex

KEY TO SHARK FAMILIES

COW AND FRILLED SHARKS pp. 24–27
6 or 7 gill slits,
anal fin,
1 dorsal fin
2 families; 4 genera

DOGFISH SHARKS pp. 28–65
5 gill slits,
no anal fin,
2 dorsal fins,
dorsal fin spines, snout short
7 families; 25 genera

SAWSHARKS pp. 66–69
5 or 6 gill slits,
no anal fin,
2 dorsal fins,
snout long and saw shaped with long barbels
1 family; 2 genera

ANGELSHARKS pp. 70–73
5 gill slits,
no anal fin,
2 dorsal fins,
body flattened, terminal mouth
1 family; 1 genus

BULLHEAD SHARKS pp. 74–77
5 gill slits,
anal fin,
2 dorsal fins,
dorsal fin spines
1 family; 1 genus

CARPETSHARKS pp. 78–99
5 gill slits,
anal fin,
2 dorsal fins,
mouth well in front of eyes
7 families; 14 genera

MACKEREL SHARKS pp. 100–121
5 gill slits,
anal fin,
2 dorsal fins,
mouth behind front of eyes,
no nictitating eyelids
7 families; 10 genera

GROUND SHARKS pp. 122–212
5 gill slits,
anal fin,
2 dorsal fins,
mouth behind front of eyes,
usually nictitating eyelids
8 families; 50 genera

KEY TO SPECIES ENTRIES

Size T total length, which is from the tip of the snout to the tip of the upper lobe of the caudal fin.

Distribution Lists the oceans and/or the countries where the species has been recorded.

Food Summarizes main diet when known. This will vary depending on season and prey availability.

Breeding Reproductive strategy (see pages 14 to 15), litter size, and gestation period when known.

Status *IUCN Red List Threatened Species Assessment* and very brief description of fisheries status when known.

COW AND FRILLED SHARKS

These sharks (order Hexanchiformes) include two distinct families; cow sharks (Hexanchidae) and frilled sharks (Chlamydoselachidae). They differ from all other living sharks by having six or seven pairs of gill slits and one dorsal fin (the Onefin Catshark is the only other living shark to have one dorsal fin). Sixgilled sharks are the oldest known living shark group, occurring all the way back to the Jurassic period. Most of the species are found worldwide, predominantly in deep cold waters of the tropics. There is some targeted fishing of these species and they are taken as bycatch in other fisheries.

There are two known species of frilled sharks, which are very similar to each other, and until recently were considered one wide-ranging species. Both have eel-like bodies and six pairs of large gills.

The four species of cow sharks are stockier than frilled sharks and have their mouths positioned under the snout. Their teeth are comblike in the lower jaw, but small and pointed in the upper; unlike the three pointed needlelike teeth of the frilled sharks.

**Frilled Shark
upper and lower teeth**

**Bluntnose Sixgill Shark
upper and lower teeth**

Frilled Shark *Chlamydoselachus anguineus*

A distinctive dark chocolate-brown to brownish-gray shark with a snakelike head and large terminal mouth. Their eyes have the brilliant green pupils often found in deepwater sharks. The Frilled Shark's small, sharp, widely spaced rows of teeth give this shark a distinctive "toothy grin."

Ranges from midwater to the bottom on offshore shelves and upper continental and island slopes, occasionally at the surface. Probably swims with its mouth open, luring prey to it with its bright white teeth.

Size The largest specimen known was a female of 77 in. TL.
Distribution Worldwide but patchily distributed. They prefer the deep waters of the outer edges of the continental shelves, but even in these areas they are rare to uncommon.
Food Deepwater actively swimming squid and fish.
Breeding Ovoviviparous, with 6–12 pups/litter. They are pregnant for a long time, probably one to two years.
Status Near threatened.

Bluntnose Sixgill Shark *Hexanchus griseus*

A large, heavy deepwater shark, it is a slow but strong swimmer. Its color is variable, anything from black to gray to tan, with a distinctive light-colored lateral line. They are often sensitive to light.

This shark is usually found between 1,640 and 3,610 ft., but it has been seen from submersibles in depths greater than 6,150 ft. The young can be seen in cold inshore waters, with adults seen by divers in shallow waters near submarine canyons.

Size They are known to reach at least 190 in. TL.
Distribution Worldwide but patchily distributed. They are usually found on shelves and slopes of continents, islands, and seamounts. Sometimes seen in shallow waters.
Food Squid, bony fish, small sharks and rays; larger sharks may feed on cetaceans and seals.
Breeding Ovoviviparous, with 22–108 pups/litter. Young and adults are thought to segregate into different habitats.
Status Near threatened. They are vulnerable to overfishing.

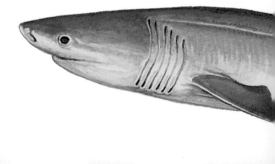

Sharpnose Sevengill Shark *Heptranchias perlo*

One of only two known sharks to have seven pairs of gill slits. They have a pointed head, a narrow mouth and large green eyes. Little is known about this shark, but captured specimens bite to defend themselves. They are thought to be strong active swimmers, sometimes swimming well off the bottom.

Mainly deepwater sharks, usually found on continental and island shelves and upper slopes, they are also found in shallower inshore waters.

Size Largest verified size is 55 in. TL, but may be larger.
Distribution It has a similar distribution to the Bluntnose Sixgill Shark, however they are usually found at shallower depths and are occasionally found inshore.
Food Bony fish, small sharks, crustaceans, squid, and cuttlefishes.
Breeding Ovoviviparous, with 6–20 pups/litter. They are thought to reproduce all year round.
Status Near threatened. Bycatch of bottom trawling and longlines has caused population declines.

DOGFISH SHARKS

A large and varied order with 106 identified shark species in seven families: Bramble sharks (Echinorhinidae)—2 species
Dogfish sharks (Squalidae)—16 species
Gulper sharks (Centrophoridae)—14 species
Lantern sharks (Etmopteridae)—41 species
Sleeper sharks (Somniosidae)—18 species
Roughsharks (Oxynotidae)—5 species
Kitefin sharks (Dalatiidae)—10 species

Their size ranges from dwarf, such as the 8 in. long Pygmy Sharks *Squaliolus* spp., to huge, for example the Pacific Sleeper Shark *Somniosus pacificus*, growing to more than 23 ft. long.

Some dogfish sharks have the oldest known age at maturity, lowest fertility (one fetus per litter in a few gulper sharks) and longest known gestation period (18–24 months for the Spurdog, *Squalus acanthias*). Many species are solitary; others form huge nomadic schools that range long distances on annual migrations. Some hunt and feed cooperatively and a few, like the cookiecutter sharks, are parasitic. The lantern sharks and other deepwater dogfish sharks have light-producing organs known as photophores. These can be seen as dark markings on their underside and are believed to be used to attract prey and for communication.

Dogfish sharks occur in a wide range of marine and estuarine habitats and depths in all oceans worldwide. They are the only sharks found in high latitudes close to the poles. Their greatest diversity occurs in deep water, many are found nowhere else, with a few species even living in depths greater than 33,000 ft. Dogfish sharks are fished commercially for meat or liver oil. Those with slow growth and low reproductive capacity are highly vulnerable to depletion by overfishing.

Bramble Shark *Echinorhinus brucus*

Body color varies from purplish gray, to brownish or blackish and is often lighter below. Some may have red or black spots or blotches on their back and sides. Edges to all fins are blackish. Its most noticeable feature is the large (greater than 0.5 in. across) sparsely and irregularly scattered whitish thornlike denticles with smooth margins. Some of these are fused into multicusped plates. The young (less than 35 in. TL) have close-set small denticles below the snout and around the mouth. These become large, scattered, and conspicuous as they mature into larger sharks.

This large shark is sluggish and is found in deepwater on continental and island shelves and slopes, on or near the bottom. It also occurs in shallow cold water upwelling areas. Other behavior is poorly known.

Size Mature: <59 in. ♂, 79–86 in. ♀. Max: 120–122 in. TL.
Distribution East Atlantic, Mediterranean, Indo-west Pacific.
Food Bony fish, small sharks, and crustaceans.
Breeding Ovoviviparous, 15–26 pups/litter.
Status Data deficient. Apparently rare, occasionally fished.

Spurdogs

Two genera, *Cirrhigaleus* (two species) and *Squalus* (14 species at least, several recently discovered and not yet described). Spurdogs are recorded almost worldwide in boreal, temperate, and most tropical seas.

They have two dorsal fins with strong ungrooved spines and no anal fin. Spurdogs' mouths are short and transverse with low bladelike cutting teeth in powerful jaws, which can dismember prey larger than themselves. Their spiracles are large and close to the eyes. The caudal peduncle has strong lateral keels and the caudal fin has no subterminal notch.

Several species are social. Some *Squalus* form huge highly nomadic schools that undertake local and long-distance annual migrations and feed communally, sometimes cleaning out or driving away local populations of prey species. Most are benthic (although some have pelagic young) and occur from the intertidal down to 1,970 ft., sometimes to 4,750 ft.

They are highly vulnerable to overfishing because of their late maturity, longevity, low fecundity, and long intervals between litters. Several stock declines have occurred and recovery of depleted populations is very slow. Many species may become threatened with extinction if restricted to small endemic or localized populations or isolated habitats. Their abundance and ease of capture make some species among the most important species targeted by commercial shark fisheries. They are landed by up to 50 countries, mostly taken in bottom-trawl fisheries. Spurdogs are of high value for their meat, liver oil, fins, and occasionally leather. Sports anglers target some species, but they are not an important game fish. A few species are regularly displayed in aquaria.

Some species use their mildly toxic fin spines and teeth for defense; a hazard to human handlers.

Piked Dogfish *Squalus acanthias*

A slender spurdog, gray to bluish gray above and lighter to white below. They often have white spots on their sides. The first dorsal fin is low with a slender, very short dorsal spine.

They are found in boreal to warm-temperate waters on continental and insular shelves, occasionally the slopes, from the surface to the bottom. They are epipelagic in cold water and usually near the bottom on continental shelves, or near the surface in oceanic waters.

Sometimes schools with other small sharks, often forming immense dense feeding aggregations on rich feeding grounds. They are slow swimmers but may undertake long-distance seasonal migrations—4,040-mile Pacific Ocean crossings have been recorded. Age at maturity, 10 to 25 years, and longevity, 70 to above 100 years, varies between populations.

Size Mature: 20.5–40 in. ♂, 26–47 in. ♀. Max: 63–79 in. TL.
Distribution Worldwide, except for tropics and near poles.
Food Mainly bony fish and invertebrates, occasionally other chondrichthyans.
Breeding Ovoviviparous, 1–32 pups/litter, varies regionally.
Status Near threatened globally (endangered northeastern Atlantic, vulnerable northwestern Atlantic). Possibly once the most abundant shark and the most important commercial species supporting large target trawl and line fisheries. Some stocks are now very seriously depleted or collapsed and catches declining steeply.

Roughskin Spurdog *Cirrhigaleus asper*

Stocky rough-skinned body with a broad flat head. The anterior nasal flaps have short stubby medial barbels. All the fins have conspicuous white edges. The dorsal fins are equally sized with very high stout spines.

Usually they occur on or near the bottom, on the upper and outer continental and insular shelves and slopes. Occasionally found off bays and river mouths. Little is known about their behavior, but their heavy body may indicate a moderately inactive benthic life.

Size Mature: 85–90 cm ♂, 89–118 cm ♀. Max: 118 cm TL.
Distribution Warm temperate to tropical west Atlantic, Indian Ocean and central Pacific.
Food Bony fish and squid.
Breeding Ovoviviparous, 18–22 pups/litter.
Status Not evaluated. Not commercially fished, probably taken as bycatch.

Longnose Spurdog *Squalus blainvillei*

Greyish-brown heavy body with a broad head. They have large medial barbels on their anterior nasal flaps. The dorsal fins are white-edged, the first dorsal fin is high and erect with a very heavy long spine.

They are found on or near muddy bottoms of continental shelves and upper slopes.

Size Mature: ~19.5 in. ♂, 23.5 in. ♀. Max: 31.5–40 in. TL.
Distribution Temperate to tropical eastern Atlantic.
Food Bony fish, crustaceans, and octopi.
Breeding Ovoviviparous, three or four pups/litter.
Status Not evaluated. Fished with other *Squalus* species.

Shortspine Spurdog *Squalus mitsukurii*

Fairly slender gray to gray-brown body, paler below and no white spots. Dorsal fins have dusky tips and an area around the caudal notch is dusky. All fins except dorsals have white posterior margins. The snout is relatively long and broad, with a large medial barbel on the anterior nasal flap. The first dorsal spine is fairly stout and short.

Occurs on or near bottom of continental and insular shelves and upper slopes, also submarine ridges and seamounts. Often in large aggregations or schools.

Size Mature: 18.5–33.5 in. ♂, 19.5–40 in. ♀. Max: 49 in. TL.
Distribution Apparently extensive and patchy.
Food Powerful predator of bony fish and invertebrates.
Breeding Ovoviviparous, 2–15 pups/litter.
Status Data deficient. Vulnerable to rapid depletion by fisheries, one population endangered.

Gulper Sharks

These are 16 mainly deepwater, bottom-dwelling species in two genera, *Centrophorus* and *Deania*. They are most diverse in warm waters and in the Indo-west Pacific.

All have huge green or yellowish eyes, bladelike teeth in both jaws, two grooved spines, and no anal fin. *Centrophorus* species have a moderate-sized snout and smoothish skin with leaf-shaped or blocklike denticles. *Deania* species have a very long snout and rough skin with tall slender dorsal dermal denticles with pitchfork-shaped crowns.

Several species are social, forming small schools or huge aggregations.

Their conservation status is mostly poorly known, but of considerable concern because rapidly expanding and unmanaged and unmonitored deepwater fisheries are now taking large numbers of these species; fisheries can cause rapid population depletion and recovery is very slow if fishing pressure is lifted. Some stocks and species are considered to be critically endangered. The Leafscale Gulper Shark is seriously depleted in the northeastern Atlantic

Gulper Shark *Centrophorus granulosus*

Typically dark gray or gray-brown above, lighter below with dusky fin webs. The free rear tips of the pectoral fins extend into acute lobes. The first dorsal fin is quite short and high, the second is similar in size. There is a shallow notch in the postventral caudal fin margin of adults.

It is found on or near the bottom on continental shelves and slopes. Not much is known about its behavior.

Size Mature: 23.5–31.5 in. ♂, >35.5 in. ♀.
Max: 41–43 in. TL.
Distribution Widespread.
Food Mainly bony fish, also squid and crustaceans.
Breeding Ovoviviparous, one or two pups/litter.
Status Vulnerable. Critically Endangered regionally off Australia,
but species identification to be confirmed. Deepwater
fisheries have caused population declines.

Leafscale Gulper Shark *Centrophorus squamosus*

Uniform gray, gray-brown or reddish-brown body with dusky
fins and rough skin, the dermal denticle crown's leaf-shaped in
adults. The pectoral fin free edges are short and not particularly
angular or elongated. The first dorsal fin is very long and low,
the second is shorter, higher, and more triangular. Posterior
margin of caudal fin slightly concave in adults.

Dermersal and pelagic over continental slopes.

Size Mature: ~40 in. ♂,
110 cm ♀. Max: 63 in. TL.
Distribution Atlantic, western Indian,
western Pacific Oceans.
Food Unknown.
Breeding Ovoviviparous, five–eight pups/litter.
Status Vulnerable. Important in several deepwater fisheries.

Birdbeak Dogfish *Deania calcea*

Fairly slender gray to dark brown body with darker colored fins; juveniles have dark posterior dorsal fin margins and dark patches above the eyes and gill regions and also on the caudal fin lobes. The skin is rough to the touch, the lateral trunk denticles are pitchfork-shaped and about $5/256$ in. long. Like other *Deania* they have extremely long flattened snouts. There is no subcaudal keel beneath caudal peduncle. They have a noticeably long, low first dorsal fin, with a shorter and taller second dorsal fin with a much longer fin spine.

This shark sometimes schools hunting for lanternfish shoals over continental and insular shelves and slopes. Other behavior is poorly known.

Size Mature: about 31.5 in. ♂, 40 in. ♀. Max: 48 in. TL.
Distribution Eastern Atlantic: Iceland to South Africa. Pacific: Japan, Taiwan Island, Australia, New Zealand, Peru to Chile.
Food Bony fish and shrimps.
Breeding Ovoviviparous, 6–12 pups/litter.
Status Least concern. Bycatch in deepwater fisheries, no declines reported.

Arrowhead Dogfish *Deania profundorum*

Fairly stocky dark gray to brown body. Dermal denticles small, $1/102$ in. long, but are rough to the touch. This is the smallest *Deania*, but still has the characteristic large green eyes and extremely long flattened snout. It is the only *Deania* with a subcaudal keel beneath the caudal peduncle. The first dorsal fin is relatively short and high, the second is much taller with a much higher fin spine.

Schools like the Birdbeak but sometimes occurs in huge aggregations on or near the bottom of the upper continental and insular slopes.

Size Mature: about 17 in. ♂, 24–31.5 in. ♀. Max: 38 in. TL.
Distribution Eastern Atlantic: western Sahara to South Africa. Western Atlantic: Gulf of Mexico and Caribbean. Indo-west Pacific: South Africa, Gulf of Aden, Philippines.
Food Small bottom and midwater bony fish, squid, and crustaceans.
Breeding Ovoviviparous, five–seven pups/litter.
Status Not evaluated. Not commercially important, probably bycaught.

Lanternsharks

The largest family of dogfish sharks, with more than 50 species in five genera; *Aculeola*, *Centroscyllium*, *Etmopterus*, *Miroscyllium*, and *Trigonognathus*. They occur almost worldwide in deepwater, some wide-ranging, but many are endemic.

New species are continually being discovered. This family includes what may be the smallest known species of sharks, the Cylindrical Lanternshark *Etmopterus carteri* and the Dwarf Lanternshark *E. perryi*, that when mature are between 4 in. and 8 in. TL.

These sharks all have photophores, either inconspicuous or forming distinct black marks on the abdomen, flanks, or tail, usually confined to or denser on the ventral surface. They have two dorsal fins with strong grooved spines, the second fin and spine usually larger. *Centroscyllium* species, comb-tooth dogfishes, have comblike teeth with cusps and cusplets in both jaws. *Aculeola*, the Hooktooth Dogfish, are very similar except for small hooklike teeth in both jaws. Lanternsharks, *Etmopterus* species, often have dark markings on their undersides. Their upper teeth have a cusp and one or more pairs of cusplets, very different in appearance to the blade-like, cutting lower teeth. Some species have lines of denticles along their flanks and dorsal surfaces that give them an engraved appearance. The Viper, *Trigonognathus*, and Rasptooth, *Miroscyllium*, Dogfish have very distinctive teeth.

Most species are bottom-dwelling in deep water, others are semioceanic. Several etmopterid dogfishes are social, and form small to huge schools or aggregations. Reproduction, where known, is ovoviviparous.

Most species are common, but poorly known. Few are large enough to be of any commercial value and most are discarded if caught as bycatch.

Black Dogfish *Centroscyllium fabricii*

Fairly stout, compressed, uniformly blackish-brown dogfish with no obvious markings. They have numerous close-set small denticles. The first dorsal fin is low with a short spine, the second dorsal fin and spine are larger. The abdomen is long with a short caudal peduncle. The mouth is distinctly curved and has comblike teeth in both jaws.

It schools over the outer continental shelves and slopes. The Black Dogfish can be closer to the surface at higher latitudes and/or in winter. Schooling is segregated by sex and size. Larger schools occur in shallower waters during the winter and spring.

Its luminescent organs are scattered, irregularly, in the skin, therefore it does not have distinct dark markings.

Size Mature: 18–19.5 in. ♂, 19.5–26 in. ♀. Max: 33– 42 in.TL.
Distribution Widespread in temperate Atlantic (tropical records uncertain).
Food Crustaceans, cephalopods, and bony fish.
Breeding Ovoviviparous, seven–eight pups/litter.
Status Not evaluated. Often abundant. Commonly discarded from fisheries bycatch.

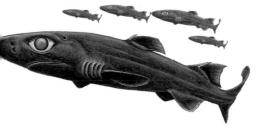

Smooth Lanternshark *Etmopterus pusillus*

A small, smooth-skinned lanternshark with a fairly slender blackish-brown body and a fairly short broad tail. There is an obscure broad black mark above, in front of, and behind the pelvic fins. The gill openings are comparatively rather long. The widely spaced, low-crowned cuspless denticles are not arranged in rows, but they do cover the snout. The second dorsal fin is less than twice the area of the first.

They live on or near the bottom of the continental slopes, but in the oceanic southern Atlantic they inhabit waters much closer to the surface. Little else is known about their behavior other than its luminescence.

Size Adults: 12–15 in. ♂, 15–18.5 in. ♀.
Max: possibly 19.5–40 in. TL.
Distribution Widespread in the Atlantic. Indo-west Pacific: South Africa and Japan.
Food Fish eggs, lanternfish, hake, squid, other small sharks.
Breeding Ovoviviparous.
Status Not evaluated. Utilized bycatch in eastern Atlantic bottom fisheries.

Velvet Belly *Etmopterus spinax*

This lanternshark has a long, fairly stout body with a long tail. It is brown above and abruptly black below, with an elongated narrow black mark above and behind the pelvic fins, others at the sides of the tail. Its gill openings are very short. There are no lines of lateral trunk denticles, but the snout is largely covered with denticles. The second dorsal fin is large, about twice the area of the first.

Found from near to well above the bottom of the outer continental shelves and upper slopes. Like most lanternsharks, due to their size and the depths they inhabit, little is known about them but for their luminescence.

Size Mature: 13–34 cm. Max: 23.5 in. TL (rare >18 in.).
Distribution Eastern Atlantic: Iceland to Gabon. Western Mediterranean.
Food Small fish, squid, and crustaceans.
Breeding Ovoviviparous, 6–20 pups/litter.
Status Not evaluated. Common. Caught offshore by bottom and pelagic trawls, used for fishmeal and food.

Hooktooth Dogfish *Aculeola nigra*

Blackish-brown stocky dogfish with broad blunt snout. Its mouth is broad and long arched with small hooklike teeth in both jaws. The gill openings are quite large. Both grooved dorsal fin spines are very short, much lower than the low dorsal fins. First dorsal fin is slightly smaller than the second. The free rear pectoral fin tips are noticeably rounded and the upper caudal lobe is long.

Not much is known about this dogfish shark, except that it is luminescent and lives a benthic and epibenthic existence above the continental shelf and upper slope.

Size Mature: 17–18 in. ♂, 20.5–21 in. ♀ TL. Max: ~23.5 in. TL.
Distribution Eastern Pacific: Peru to Chile.
Food Not known.
Breeding Ovoviviparous, at least three pups/litter.
Status Data deficient. Relatively common within limited range, possibly fisheries bycatch.

Rasptooth Dogfish *Miroscyllium sheikoi*

This is one lanternshark that can be easily distinguished from other lanternsharks. It is black below and dark brown above with black photomarks on the caudal peduncle and the caudal fin. All fins have pale to white posterior margins. The long flat snout is unmistakable. The mouth is short and has small comblike compressed teeth with cusps and cusplets in both jaws. The dorsal fin spines are grooved, the second is much larger than the first.

Little is known about this lanternshark other than it is luminescent and inhabits the upper slopes of a single submarine ridge.

Size Mature: between 12–15.75 in. TL ♂. Max: at least 17 in. TL.
Distribution Northwesteern Pacific, near Japan.
Food Not known.
Breeding Probably ovoviviparous.
Status Data deficient. Of no commercial value but could be taken by deepwater trawls.

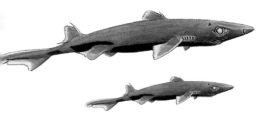

Green Lanternshark *Etmopterus virens*

This dwarf dark brown or gray-black, moderately slender lanternshark has a long narrow tail with a dorsal margin as long as its head. There are elongated broad black marks above and behind the pelvic fins and others at the tail base and along the tail's axis. The underside is also black. Its gill openings are very short, less than one-third the length of its eye. The upper teeth generally have less than three pairs of cusplets. Lateral trunk denticles are very short, stout, hooked, and with conical crowns. They are widely spaced, but are not in rows. Denticles also cover the snout area. The second dorsal fin is comparatively large and over twice the area of the first.

Other than being luminescent and found on the upper continental slopes, little else is known about this lanternshark.

Size Mature: 7in. ♂, 8.5 in. ♀. Max: 10 in. TL.
Distribution Northwestern Atlantic: northern Gulf of Mexico and Caribbean, possibly Brazil.
Food May school and communally attack very large prey (squid).
Breeding Presumably ovoviviparous.
Status Least concern. Relatively common. Discarded bycatch.

Viper Dogfish *Trigonognathus kabeyai*

An unmistakable lanternshark with very long, narrow, snakelike mouth, and huge curved fanglike teeth in front of both highly protrusible jaws. There are deep pockets around the front of the upper jaws and very large diagonally elongated spiracles behind its large eyes. Both dorsal fins have grooved spines, the second being much longer than the first. Its body is dark brown above and black below, with black photomarks on the caudal peduncle and the caudal fin.

It is apparently luminescent and found on the bottom of the upper continental slopes. On the uppermost slopes of seamount they occur around 890 ft. deep. They could possibly be also oceanic. Nothing is really known about its behavior or biology.

Size Mature: 14.5–17 in. ♂, >17 in. TL ♀. Max: at least 17 in. TL.
Distribution Northern and central Pacific, Japan, and on record from the Hawaiian Islands.
Food Long narrow jaws can probably be protruded to impale relatively large prey (bony fishes and crustaceans) on fanglike teeth, then swallowed whole.
Breeding Possibly ovoviviparous.
Status Data deficient. Apparently rare and localized.

Sleeper Sharks

This family consists of eighteen deepwater, benthic, and oceanic species in seven genera; *Centroscymnus*, *Centroselachus*, *Proscymnodon*, *Scymnodalatias*, *Scymnodon*, *Somniosus*, and *Zameus*. They occur circumglobally in most seas, from the tropics to the Arctic and Antarctic oceans. Some are small, 16 to 27 in., others gigantic, greater than 20 ft. in length.

They have fairly broad heads with flat snouts and short thin-lipped, almost transverse mouths. Their spiracles are large and close behind the eyes. Lateral ridges run along the abdomen, but not usually on the caudal peduncle, except in most *Somniosus*. They have two small broad dorsal fins with the second usually smaller or the same size as the first. Some species have spines on both fins, which may be covered by skin, but these are absent in *Scymnodalatias* and *Somniosus*.

Most species occur near the seabed on continental and insular slopes from 656 ft. to at least 12,060 ft. and a few species are oceanic or semioceanic. In high northern latitudes the Greenland and Pacific Sleeper Sharks occur on continental shelves and can even be found in the intertidal regions and at the surface. Sleeper sharks feed on bony fishes, other sharks, rays and chimaeras, cephalopods and other mollusks, crustaceans, seals, whale meat carrion, marine birds, echinoderms, and jellyfish.

They are an important component of commercial targeted and bycatch deepwater shark fisheries. They are used for food or fishmeal and their large very oily livers are processed for their high squalene content. Their conservation status is poorly known, but of considerable concern because expanding deepwater fisheries are now taking large numbers of deepwater sharks. Their life history is sketchily known, but it is suspected that their reproductive capacity is limited and growth slow. If so, these species are highly vulnerable to overfishing.

Portuguese Dogfish *Centroscymnus coelolepis*

A uniformly blackish to golden-brown, stocky, short-snouted dogfish. It has a large mouth with short labial furrows. Its upper teeth are slender; the broader, lower teeth have short bent cusps. The adults have large, round, flat overlapping denticles making the skin feel smooth. They do have spines but these are very small and may be covered by skin. The dorsal fins are small and equal-sized, the second being close to the asymmetrical caudal fin.

They hunt on or near the bottom of the continental slopes and upper and middle abyssal plain rises. Sometimes they feed by taking bites out of live prey, like the cookiecutter sharks, *Isistius*.

Size Mature: ~31.5 in. ♂, 40 in. ♀. Max: ~47 in. TL.
Distribution Atlantic, Indian, and Pacific Oceans.
Food Bony fish, other sharks, benthic invertebrates, and cetacean and seal meat.
Breeding Ovoviviparous, 13–17 pups/litter.
Status Near threatened. Long history of bycatch and target deepwater fisheries, used for fishmeal and squalene from liver oil. Seriously depleted in the northeastern Atlantic.

Longnose Velvet Dogfish
Centroselachus crepidater

Slender, black to dark brown dogfish with narrow light posterior fin margins. The snout is very long, as are the upper labial furrows, which almost encircle the small mouth. The denticles are round, flat, and overlapping with triple cusps on their crowns in adults. They have roughly equally sized dorsal fins with very small spine tips protruding from the skin. The first dorsal fin base is extended forward as a prominent ridge, which begins directly over the pectoral fin bases.

Their behavior is not known, other than they live on or near the bottom of the upper continental and insular slopes.

Size Mature: ~25–27 in. ♂, 32 in. ♀. Max: 41 in. TL.
Distribution Eastern Atlantic, Indo-Pacific, not northeastern Pacific.
Food Fish and cephalopods.
Breeding Ovoviviparous, four–eight pups/litter, breeds year-round.
Status Least concern. Common and wide-ranging. Limited but increasing fisheries interest, bycatch utilized for fishmeal and liver oil.

Knifetooth Dogfish *Scymnodon ringens*

This rather aggressive-looking, uniformly black dogfish has no obvious fin markings. It has a rather thick, high head with a broad short snout. The mouth is very large and broadly arched. Its teeth are asymmetric; the upper teeth are small and lanceolate, the lower teeth, however, are huge triangular-shaped cutting teeth. The gill slits are somewhat long, greater than half the eye length. The dorsal fin spines are tiny, with the second dorsal fin slightly larger than the first. Its caudal fin is asymmetric with no lower lobe.

Its comparatively immense, triangular, razor-edged lower teeth suggest that this is a formidable predator, probably capable of attacking and dismembering large prey. It is found on continental slopes, on or near the bottom.

Size Max: ~43 in. TL.
Distribution Eastern Atlantic: Scotland to Senegal. West Pacific: New Zealand?
Food Not known.
Breeding Probably ovoviviparous.
Status Not evaluated. Relatively common in eastern Atlantic. Bycatch of bottom trawls, line gear, and fixed bottom nets; dried-salted for food and fishmeal.

Plunket's Shark *Proscymnodon plunketi*

A dark gray-brown, very short-snouted dogfish with a stocky body that tapers behind the pectoral fins. It has roughly equal-sized dorsal fins with the tips of the spines just protruding through the skin. The first dorsal fin base extends forward in a prominent ridge. Its pectoral fins are broad with rounded margins.

This dogfish is found near the bottom of continental and insular slopes. It is known to form large schools that are segregated by size and sex and may be vulnerable to fisheries.

Size Mature: 40–51.5 in. ♂, 50.75 in. ♀. Max: 67 in. TL.
Distribution Indo-Pacific: Australasia and southwestern Indian Ocean, possibly southern Africa.
Food Cephalopods and bony fish.
Breeding Ovoviviparous, up to 36 pups/litter.
Status Near threatened. Relatively uncommon. Deepwater fisheries bycatch, used in New Zealand for fish meal and squalene.

Whitetail Dogfish *Scymnodalatias albicauda*

This dogfish has a dark brown or mottled grayish body, which is lighter below. Its fin margins are whitish-gray and there are obvious white blotches on the caudal fin. The snout is short, broad, and rounded. Its eyes are horizontally elongated, but not slitlike. The mouth is long and broadly arched with small upper teeth that have very narrow acute erect cusps. The lower teeth are larger, unserrated, and blade-like with high, erect cusps. Its pectoral fins are elongated and there are no dorsal fin spines. The second dorsal fin is slightly larger than the first and very close to the tail.

It is possibly mesopelagic or bathypelagic, living in the oceanic and epipelagic zone. They are found near the bottom on submarine ridges, at about 1,640 ft. It is thought that they may rise near to the surface at night.

Size Born: >8 in. TL. Adult ♀: 29–43 in. TL.
Distribution Southern Ocean.
Food Not known.
Breeding Ovoviviparous, very large litters: at least 59 pups/litter.
Status Data deficient. Very rarely caught by deepwater trawls and tuna longlines.

Velvet Dogfish *Zameus squamulosus*

Small slender black dogfish with low, flat head and fairly long, narrow snout. Its mouth is short and narrow. The small spearlike upper teeth are high-cusped, but the lower teeth are knifelike. The skin is quite rough to the touch with the denticles being tricuspidate with transverse ridges. The two dorsal fins have small fin spines, the second dorsal fin is larger, and about the same size as the small pelvic fins. It has a long tail with a strong subterminal tail notch and a short lower lobe.

Little is known about this dogfish other than it lives on or near the bottom of the continental and insular slopes. It is epipelagic and oceanic off the coast of Brazil and the Hawaiian Islands.

Size Adults: 19–20 cm ♂, 23–27 in. ♀. Max: 27 in. TL.
Distribution Patchy worldwide, not eastern Pacific.
Food Not known.
Breeding Probably ovoviviparous.
Status Data deficient. Minor bycatch in bottom fisheries. Used dried-salted for food and as fishmeal. Formerly recognized as *Scymnodon obscurus* in eastern Atlantic.

Little Sleeper Shark *Somniosus rostratus*

A small, uniformly dark to blackish sleeper shark. It has a short, rounded snout and short head on a cylindrical body. The spearlike upper teeth are different to the larger slicing lowers with their high semierect cusps and low roots. Its skin is smooth, because it has flat cusped denticles. The dorsal fins are spineless, the first being higher, and closer to the pectoral fins than the pelvic fins. It has a short caudal peduncle with lateral keels on the caudal fin base. The fin itself has a long lower caudal lobe and a short upper lobe.

It has been found on or near the bottom on the outer continental shelves, upper and lower slopes. Little else is known.

Size Mature: ~27.5 in. ♂, 31.5 in. ♀. Max: 55 in. TL.
Distribution Northeastern Atlantic, western Mediterranean, northwestern Atlantic (Cuba).
Food Not known.
Breeding Ovoviviparous.
Status Not evaluated. Rare to sporadically common. Minimal fisheries interest, caught on longlines and by bottom trawls, used for fishmeal and possibly food.

Greenland Shark *Somniosus microcephalus*

A gigantic, medium gray or brown, heavy-bodied sleeper shark, which sometimes has transverse dark bands. The skin is rough to the touch, because the denticles have strong hook-like erect cusps. Its low, equal-sized dorsal fins have no spines. It also has lateral keels present on the base of caudal fin.

This is a sluggish shark that offers little resistance to capture and is easily fished through iceholes. It has a highly conspicuous, possibly luminescent, copepod parasite often attached to the cornea of the eye, which is speculated to lure prey species to the shark under a mutualistic and beneficial relationship. They occur over continental and insular shelves and upper slopes to at least 4,000 ft. deep in water temperatures between 33 and 53°F. They may move into shallower waters in spring and summer in the northern Atlantic.

Size Most adults: 96–168 in. Max: >252 in., possibly 287 in. TL.
Distribution North Atlantic and Arctic, occasionally to Portugal.
Food Able to capture large, active prey including fish, invertebrates, seabirds, and seals. Also feeds on dead cetaceans, drowned horses, and reindeer.
Breeding Ovoviviparous, 10 pups/litter.
Status Near Threatened. Abundant. Traditionally fished by hook and line, longline, or gaff for liver oil. Meat toxic when fresh, unless washed. Considered harmless.

Pacific Sleeper Shark *Somniosus pacificus*

A giant sleeper shark with uniform grayish body and fins. The skin is rough and bristly to the touch, as the denticles have strong hooklike erect cusps. The dorsal fins are similar to the Greenland Shark, but the first dorsal fin is slightly closer to the pelvic fins than to pectoral fins, which is the opposite in the Greenland Shark. It has a short caudal peduncle, with lateral keels variably present or absent on the base of the caudal fin.

This is a lumbering sluggish shark. Its small mouth and large oral cavity suggest suction feeding. They may be sexually segregated, but pregnant females have not been recorded. They are found over continental shelves and slopes, to over 6,560 ft. They have also been found in the littoral zone in northern parts of their range; one was found trapped in a tide pool. Lives in very deep water in the southern part of its distribution.

Size Adult ♀: 146–169 in. TL. Max: >276 in. TL.
Distribution North Pacific: Japan to Mexico.
Food Takes a wide variety of surface and bottom animals. Seal remains found in stomach may be either scavenged carrion or taken alive.
Breeding Probably ovoviviparous; up to 300 large eggs/female.
Status Not evaluated. Relatively common.

Roughsharks

In this family there are five unmistakable species of small shark. They all have compressed bodies, triangular in cross section, with lateral ridges on the abdomen. Their rough skin, which gives them their name, is from large, prickly, and close-set denticles. The two high sail-like dorsal fins are spined. They have rather broad, flattened heads with flat, blunt snouts and small thick-lipped mouths encircled by elongated labial furrows. The large nostrils are close-set. Their spiracles are large to enormous and placed close behind the eyes. The small, spearlike upper teeth form a triangular pad; the lower teeth are highly compressed, forming a sawlike cutting edge, with only 9 to 13 rows of teeth. They have no anal fin.

Like most deepwater sharks, little is known about them. They have a scattered distribution, mainly on temperate to tropical continental and island shelves. It is thought that they are weak swimmers, relying on their large oily livers for buoyancy. They mainly feed on small bottom-living invertebrates, like worms, crustaceans, and mollusks, as well as fish. Females bear litters of between 7 and 23 pups. Uncommon bycatch in deepwater bottom fisheries. May be processed for fish meal, liver oil or occasionally human food.

Headon view of an Angular Roughshark

Angular Roughshark *Oxynotus centrina*

This is a gray or gray-brown roughshark with darker blotches on the head and sides, which are not always conspicuous in adults. There is also a light horizontal line that crosses the cheek below the eye. It has ridges over the eyes that are expanded into huge rounded knobs, which are covered with enlarged denticles, which is absent in other roughsharks. The spiracles are very large and vertically elongated, and are almost as high as its eye length. The first dorsal spine leans slightly forward.

They are to be found on coralline, algae covered and muddy bottoms on continental shelves and upper slopes. Very little is known about their behavior.

Size Mature: ~19.5 in. Most records <39 in. Max: ~59 in. TL.
Distribution Eastern Atlantic and Mediterranean (not Black Sea); possibly off Mozambique, West Indian Ocean.
Food Worms, crustaceans, and mollusks.
Breeding Litter size 7–8 (Angola) to 23 (Mediterranean).
Status Not evaluated. Rare to uncommon. Minor offshore trawl bycatch.

Kitefin Sharks

In this family there are ten species in seven genera of dwarf to medium-sized deepwater sharks; *Dalatias*, *Euprotomicroides*, *Euprotomicrus*, *Heteroscymnoides*, *Isistius*, *Squaliolus*, *Mollisquama*. They are distributed almost world-wide, in open ocean or on the bottom, in mostly temperate to tropical seas. Some species are wide ranging, others restricted to single ocean basins or ridges, but may prove to be more widespread with additional sampling.

Their heads are narrow and conical and the snout is short. Their strong jaws have small spearlike upper teeth and large bladelike interlocked lower teeth with smooth or serrated (*Dalatias* only) edges. The pectoral fins are short with broadly rounded free rear tips. Their two dorsal fins are without fin spines or only with a first dorsal fin spine (*Squaliolus* species). The second dorsal fin varies from slightly smaller to much larger than first. There is no anal fin. Their caudal fins have long upper lobes and long to very short, or even absent, lower lobes with well developed subterminal notches.

Their biology is poorly known. They are ovoviviparous, aplacental viviparous, with up to 6 to 16 pups/litter in larger species. Some species are powerful predators, others are ectoparasites; some are solitary and others occur in aggregations for at least part of their lifecycle. The Kitefin Shark is important in target and bycatch fisheries for meat, used for human consumption and/or fishmeal, and for the squalene oil from their large livers. Other species are too small to be of commercial value.

Kitefin Shark *Dalatias licha*

A medium-sized, cylindrical, brown to blackish shark with a short blunt snout. The mouth has thick, fringed lips and serrated lower teeth. Its dorsal fins are spineless, with the first originating behind the pectoral fin rear tips. The base of the first dorsal is closer to the pectoral fin than to pelvic fin bases, and the second dorsal fin is larger. Its ventral caudal fin lobe is weak. The posterior margins of most fins are translucent.

They are known to hover above the bottom using their large oil-filled livers to provide neutral buoyancy. They are also found swimming well off the bottom. They are a deepwater shark. They range usually on or near the bottom of warm-temperate and tropical waters over outer continental and insular shelves and slopes.

Size Mature: 30–47.5 in. ♂, 46–62.5 in. ♀. Max: 62.5–71.5 in. TL.
Distribution Atlantic, Indian, and Pacific Oceans.
Food Solitary hunter of mainly deepwater fish, may take bites out of large live prey.
Breeding Ovoviviparous, 10–16 pups/litter.
Status Data deficient. Near threatened in northeastern Atlantic. Fisheries for meat and squalene may deplete populations rapidly.

Cookiecutter Shark *Isistius brasiliensis*

A small, medium gray or gray-brown cigar-shaped shark, with light-edged fins and prominent dark collar mark around the throat. The lower teeth are large and triangular in 25 to 31 rows surrounded by suctorial lips. The dorsal fins are set far back near the large, nearly symmetrical paddle-shaped caudal fin. It has luminous organs covering the lower surface (except for the fins and the collar), which glow bright green.

It is a wide-ranging tropical oceanic shark. They have only been caught at night, sometimes at the surface but usually in deeper in water, 279 to 11,500 ft., and frequently near islands, possibly at pupping grounds or concentrations of prey.

They are poor swimmers and probably migrate vertically from deep waters, to midwater or the surface at night. They are an ectoparasite on large fish and cetaceans, which are possibly lured to the shark by its bioluminescent light organs. Its thick lips and modified pharynx are used to attach itself to the prey. See page 14.

Size Mature: ~12–14.5 in. ♂,
14–17 in. ♀. Max: >15 in. ♂, >19.5 in. TL ♀.
Distribution Atlantic, southern Indian Ocean, and Pacific.
Food Deepwater fish, squid, and crustaceans.
Breeding Presumably ovoviviparous, about six–seven pups/litter.
Status Least concern. Too small to be taken by most fisheries, but occasional bycatch.

Largetooth Cookiecutter Shark *Isistius plutodus*

This species has larger jaws and a bigger mouth than other cookiecutter sharks. It has only 17 to 19 rows of lower teeth, but they are enormous. The eyes are set well forward on the short-snouted head to provide binocular vision. They have no collar markings at all on the throat. The asymmetric caudal fin is small with a short ventral lobe.

Like the Cookiecutter they are epipelagic and possibly bathypelagic, but in shallower waters. They are only known from a few scattered localities near land.

Their smaller fins suggest that they are less active swimmers than the Cookiecutter Shark. Not much is known about this species but they are probably similar to the Cookiecutter in having large, oil-filled livers and body cavity to provide neutral buoyancy, or in compensation for a highly calcified skeleton. The lower teeth are swallowed, as they are replaced in rows, which, perhaps, is to recycle the calcium. Cookiecutters have been reported to attack rubber sonar domes on nuclear submarines. Cookiecutters can be active and bite when caught.

Size Max: at least 17 in. TL.
Distribution Western Atlantic,
northeastern Atlantic, western Pacific.
Food Takes even larger and more elongated
bites (twice as long as diameter of mouth) out
of bony fish than the Cookiecutter, and may
do likewise to other prey
Breeding Not known.
Status Least concern.

Pygmy Shark *Euprotomicrus bispinatus*

A tiny cylindrical black shark with a bulbous snout, large eyes, and light-edged fins. They have luminous organs on the underside of their body. Gill slits are tiny. The caudal peduncle has low lateral keels. The tiny flaglike first dorsal fin is one-quarter the length of the second and well behind the pectoral fins. Its caudal fin is nearly symmetrical and paddle-shaped.

They are epipelagic, mesopelagic, and, perhaps, bathypelagic in deep midocean. Like many similar species they migrate from the surface at night to deeper than 4,900 ft., at least to midwater and perhaps the bottom by day.

Size Born: 2.5–4 in. TL. Mature: 6.5–7.5 in. ♂, 8.5–9 in. ♀. Max: 10.5 in. TL.
Distribution Oceanic and amphitemperate. South Atlantic, southern Indian and Pacific Oceans.
Food Deepwater squid, bony fish, some crustaceans, not large prey.
Breeding Ovoviviparous, eight pups/litter.
Status Least concern.

Smalleye Pygmy Shark *Squaliolus aliae*

This is a spindle-shaped, blackish dwarf shark with a long, bulbous, conical snout and prominent light fin margins. There is a fin spine, sometimes covered by skin, only on the first dorsal fin, the origin of which is opposite the inner margins or rear tips of pectoral fins. The second dorsal fin base is more than twice the length of the first. The caudal fin is paddle-shaped. The eye is smaller than the very similar Spined Pygmy Shark, *Squaliolus laticaudus*, and the upper eyelid is angular. There are a pair of tiny lateral papillae on the upper lip, which partially cover the teeth. Their ventral surface is covered with photophores.

Their biology is virtually unknown. They are thought to migrate daily from shallow depths at night to deeper water by day. They are known to be epipelagic or mesopelagic near land.

Size One of the smallest living sharks. Mature: ~6 in. ♂. Max: ~8.5 in. TL.
Distribution Southeastern Indian Ocean and western Pacific.
Food Not known.
Breeding Ovoviviparous, litter size unknown.
Status Least concern. Wide ranging, considered too small by some authorities to be threatened by fisheries, but a common bycatch of bottom-trawl fisheries in the western Pacific.

Taillight Shark *Euprotomicroides zantedeschia*

Only known from two specimens. A blackish-brown shark with a very wide fifth gill slit, more than twice the length of the first. The cloaca is greatly expanded as a luminous gland containing yellow papillae. One was caught in a bottom trawl on the continental shelf, the other near the surface far offshore.

Size Immature ♀: 7 in. TL.
Adult ♂: 16 in. TL.
Distribution South Atlantic.
Food Unknown.
Breeding Unknown,
probably ovoviviparous.
Status Data deficient.

Longnose Pygmy Shark *Heteroscymnoides marleyi*

A dark brown dwarf shark with a very long bulbous snout and small gill slits. It lives in the epipelagic zone in cold, sub-antarctic oceanic waters and cold current systems (Benguela and Humboldt).

Size Mature ♀: 13 in. TL. Max: ~14.5 in. TL ♂.
Distribution Southern Ocean. Possibly circumglobal.
Food Like above, unknown.
Breeding Presumably ovoviviparous, likely small litters.
Status Least concern. Only six specimens recorded.

Pocket Shark *Mollisquama parini*

small, dark brown shark with a short, blunt, conical snout
and thick, fringed lips. There is a large pocketlike gland with
a conspicuous slitlike opening just above each pectoral fin
base, which possibly secretes a pheromone or luminous fluid.
The fins are dark with light margins. It has medium-sized
gill slits with the fifth gill slit almost twice the length of the
first. Its first dorsal fin is well behind the pectoral fins and the
base is just in front of the pelvic fin bases. The second dorsal
fin is about as large as the first. The caudal fin is asymmetrical
and not paddle-shaped, with a weak lower lobe.

Only known from one specimen that was caught on the
Nasca submarine ridge, about 745 miles east of Chile, at a
depth of 1,083 ft.

Size Max: over 15.75 in. TL (adolescent ♀).
Distribution Southeastern Pacific.
Food Not known.
Breeding Not known.
Status Data deficient.

SAWSHARKS

This order (Pristiophormes) contains one family of little-known small sharks. Once distributed worldwide in the fossil record, they are now found only on the continental and insular shelves and upper slopes of the northwestern and southeastern Atlantic, western Indian and western Pacific Oceans, in shallow water in temperate regions, deeper in the tropics. Sometimes found in large schools or feeding in aggregations. At least one species is segregated by depth, with adults found in deeper water than the young. Some have a very restricted distribution.

They are small slender sharks (max. ~59 in. TL, most <27.5 in.) with cylindrical bodies, flattened heads, and a long flat sawlike snout with a pair of long stringlike ventral barbels in front of the nostrils and close-set rows of lateral and ventral sawteeth. Eyes are on the side of the head, with large spiracles. There are thick lateral ridges on the caudal peduncle. They may be confused with the sawfishes, which are rays or batoids, but these all have flattened bodies, pectoral fins fused to the head, and the gill slits are underneath the head.

The large lateral rostral teeth erupt before birth but lie flat against the rostrum of the young until after birth. The tooth-studded rostrum has sensors to detect vibrations and electric fields, and is probably used to capture and kill prey. It may also be used for defense, or when competing or courting with other sawsharks. The long rostral barbels may have taste, touch, or other sensors and are trailed along the bottom to locate prey, including small fish, crustaceans, and squid.

They are harmless to man, despite very sharp teeth. They are very vulnerable to bycatch if a restricted range coincides with fisheries; their saws may easily be entangled in fishing gear, including nets. The saws may also be sold as curios.

Sixgill Sawshark *Pliotrema warreni*

This is the only sawshark with six pairs of gill slits and the only other shark with more than five pairs of gill slits, other than the frilled or cow sharks. There are barbs on the posterior edges of the larger rostral sawteeth, which are absent in other sawsharks. The barbels are also closer to the mouth than in the other species.

Sixgill Sawsharks are found on or near the bottom of offshore continental shelves and upper slopes. The adults live deeper than the pups. They are thought to use inshore pupping grounds.

One of their main predators is the Tiger Shark.

Size Mature: ~32.5 in. ♂, ~43 in. ♀. Max: 44 in. ♂, >53.5 in. TL ♀.
Distribution Southeastern Atlantic (South Africa), southwestern Indian Ocean (South Africa, southern Mozambique, southeastern Madagascar).
Food Small fish, crustaceans, and squid.
Breeding Five–seven pups/litter, 7–17 developing eggs/female.
Status Near threatened. Uncommon and localized in distribution. Discarded bycatch from bottom-trawl fisheries.

Bahamas Sawshark *Pristiophorus schroederi*

A slender, uniform light gray sawshark with a whitish underside. There are darker brownish stripes along the rostrum midline and edges. The pectoral fins have light edges, with the juveniles having a dark anterior edge to the dorsal fins. The rostrum is very long, narrow, and tapering, the preoral length being 31–32% of the total length. The barbels are found halfway between the mouth and the rostral tip. The edge of the rostrum is concave around the prebarbel area, with 23 large, lateral sawteeth in total along its length, 13 before and 10 behind the barbels. Juveniles usually have one smaller tooth between every large lateral tooth.

These sharks are found on or near the bottom of continental and insular slopes. Little else is known about the behavior of this shark.

Size Max: >32 in. TL.
Distribution Northwestern Atlantic: between Cuba, Florida, and Bahamas.
Food Not known.
Breeding Not known.
Status Data deficient. Possibly bycatch of deepwater fisheries

Dwarf Sawshark *Pristiophorus* sp. D

These are very small, uniformly brown sawsharks with a white underside and a pale rostrum, with dark brown stripes on middle and edges. The first dorsal fin is broad and triangular with its rear tip extending behind the pelvic fin midbases. The pectoral and dorsal fins have dark anterior margins, which are more obvious in juveniles, and prominent, light, trailing edges. There are prominent ridges on the bases of the large lateral rostral teeth. There are two rows of four or five enlarged pits on the underside, prebarbel, of the rostrum. Its barbels are much closer to the mouth than to the rostral tip.

Little is known about this large green-eyed sawshark other than it has been found on the upper continental slope.

Size Mature: ~18–19.5 in. ♂, 22 in. ♀. Max: >24 in. TL.
Distribution Western Indian Ocean: Mozambique, possibly Somalia, to the Arabian Sea off Pakistan.
Food Not known.
Breeding Not known.
Status Least concern. Occurs in very deep water not currently commercially fished.

ANGELSHARKS

Called Monkfish by Guillame Rondelet in 1555, for their monklike silhouette. They are found mainly on mud and sand on cool temperate continental shelves, from intertidal to continental slopes and deeper in tropical waters. They are absent from most of the Indian Ocean and central Pacific.

These medium-sized sharks (order Squatiformes) look similar to rays, with a broad flattened body, short snout, and large fins, but the gill openings are on the sides of the head, not beneath as in the rays. Also, the very large pectoral fins are not attached to the head, like rays, but the gill openings are in front of the pectoral fin origins and are covered by the triangular anterior fin lobes. The eyes are on top of the head, close to the large spiracles. Their large mouths and nostrils are at the front of the snout, the mouth extending at the sides to opposite or slightly behind the eyes. The two spineless dorsal fins are set back on the precaudal tail. The short, very thick keels are at the base of the caudal peduncle with the caudal fin having a longer ventral lobe than the anterior.

Their reproduction is ovoviviparous, with litters of 1–25 pups. They are often found lying buried by day in the mud and sand, with their eyes and spiracles showing. They are ambush feeders, using their unusually flexible "necks" to raise their heads and protruding traplike jaws to snap up prey at high speed. They do not swim far and populations may easily be isolated by deepwater or areas of unsuitable habitat.

They are harmless, unless disturbed or provoked. Many species are intensively fished for food, oil, fishmeal, and leather. All are very vulnerable target and bycatch species in bottom fisheries. There are significant population reductions reported for many heavily fished species. Recolonization of depleted populations from adjacent areas may be very slow

Angelshark *Squatina squatina*

This is a very large and stocky angelshark. Its color is variable from gray to reddish or greenish brown, with scattered small white spots and blackish dots and spots. A white nuchal spot may be present but there are no ocelli. Young often have white reticulations and large dark blotches. The nasal barbels are simple, with straight or spatulate tips. The small thorns on the middle of the back in young disappear with age, but the skin remains very rough. On the snout and between the eyes there are patches of small thorns.

Angelsharks lie buried with their eyes protruding, by day, but swim strongly off the bottom at night. They seasonally migrate into colder water in the summer. They are found on mud or sand bottoms from inshore on coasts and estuaries, but deeper on the continental shelf.

Size Mature: 49.5–66 in. ♀. Max: 72 in. ♂, possibly to 96 in. TL ♀.
Distribution Northeastern Atlantic: historically from Norway to Mauritania, Canary Islands, Mediterranean, and Black Sea, now extinct in the North Sea and vanished from other areas.
Food Mainly flatfishes, skate, crustaceans, and mollusks. One record of a cormorant swallowed.
Breeding 7–25 pups/litter, increasing with female size.
Status Endangered. Range and abundance declining severely.

Pacific Angelshark *Squatina californica*

A reddish-brown to dark brown, or even blackish angelshark with scattered light spots set around dark blotches in the adult. In the young, large, paired dark blotches on the back and the tail form large ocelli. The pectoral and pelvic fins are white edged. Its nasal barbels are conical and simple with spatulate tips. The anterior nasal flaps are weakly fringed and there are no triangular lobes on the lateral head folds. Its head dips concavely between the large eyes. Thorns are prominent in the young, but are small or absent in the adults.

It lies buried in flat sand or mud by day on the continental shelf, often around rocks and sometimes near kelp beds. It is an ambush hunter and is more active at night although, even then, it does not swim long distances.

Size Born: 10–10.5 in. TL. Mature: ~39 in. (California, smaller in Mexico). Max: 47–60 in. TL.
Distribution Northeastern Pacific, possibly southeastern Pacific.
Food Not known.
Breeding 6–10 pups/litter after nine to ten month gestation. About 20% survive to maturity at 10–13 years old.
Status Near threatened. Abundant in California until fishery for meat caused population collapse in early 1990s. Gill-net ban ended fishery. Taken as bycatch elsewhere.

Sand Devil *Squatina dumeril*

This is an almost plain bluish to ashy-gray angelshark with only dusky or blackish spots, irregularly present or absent. Small white spots are often present in the young. The underside is white with red spots and reddish fin margins. The dorsal fins' rear tips are light. Its nasal barbels are simple and tapering, with weakly fringed or smooth anterior nasal flaps. The lateral head folds are low and have no triangular lobes. Its head is strongly concave between the large eyes. There are a few small but prominent thorns on the snout, between the eyes and the spiracles in the young. In adults they are more numerous and form patches. The thorns along the back of the young are reduced and inconspicuous in the adults.

Sand Devils are found on or near the bottom of the continental shelf and slope. They appear in inshore shallow waters in the spring and summer off the U.S. and disappear, probably into deeper water, in the winter.

Size Mature: 36–42 in. ♂. Max: 60 in. TL.
Distribution Northwestern Atlantic: New England to Gulf of Mexico. Unconfirmed: Cuba, Nicaragua, Jamaica, and Venezuela.
Food Small bottom fish, crustaceans, and bivalves.
Breeding Up to 25 pups/litter born in summer.
Status Data deficient. Not targeted by fisheries, some bycatch. Aggressive when captured.

BULLHEAD SHARKS

This is an ancient order (Herodontiformes) with a long fossil record, almost to the beginning of the Mezozoic Era, but now only represented by one living family. The taxonomic name *Heterodontus* means "different teeth." This is shown by the front small, pointed, holding teeth and the rear large, blunt teeth used for crushing their prey, mainly invertebrates.

They are small, mostly less than 39 in., stout-bodied sharks, with two, spined dorsal fins and an anal fin. They all have blunt, "piglike" snouts, small mouths, enlarged first gill slits, prominent eye ridges, and rough skin.

All are sluggish, nocturnal, benthic sharks. Usually swimming slowly or crawling over rocky, kelp-covered or sandy bottoms. Some rest by day in rocky crevices and caves. They lay unique, large, screw-shaped eggcases that often become lodged firmly in crevices on the bottom. The large young do not hatch until after five months or more. At least two species lay eggs in particular "nesting" sites, another is migratory when adult, returning each year after long migrations to its breeding sites. The majority have restricted distributions. They mainly feed on benthic invertebrates such as sea urchins, crabs, shrimps, gastropods, oysters, and worms, but rarely on small fish.

They are rare to uncommon, and are not important to commercial fisheries, but are often taken as bycatch. They are also caught by sport anglers and divers.

Port Jackson Shark egg case

Horn Shark egg case

Zebra Bullhead Shark egg case

Port Jackson Shark *Heterodontus portusjacksoni*

This shark is gray to light brown or even whitish, with unique distinctive dark "harness" markings and a dark band between and under the eyes.

It occurs in temperate waters, from the intertidal zone to at least 900 ft. deep. Here it rests by day in groups on sandy-bottomed caves and gullies. It uses traditional collective egg-laying sites. The hatchlings move to nearby nursery grounds until adolescent, when they move again, well offshore, segregated by sex, and join the adult population a few years later. Adults also segregate by sex and undertake complex seasonal breeding migrations.

Size Egg case: 5–7 long x 2–2.5 in. (broad end). Mature: 27.5–31.5 in. ♂, 31.5–37 in. ♀. Max: 65 (rare >93) in. TL.
Distribution Southern Australia. One New Zealand record.
Food Mainly sea urchins, other benthic invertebrates, also small fish.
Breeding Mating and egg-laying occurs mainly in August–September. Eggs hatch 12 months later.
Status Least concern. Abundant. Taken as bycatch but mostly returned alive.

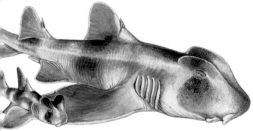

Horn Shark *Heterodontus francisci*

A dark to light gray or brown shark, usually with small dark spots. Below the eye there is a dusky patch, also with small dark spots. The young are more brightly colored, with obvious dark saddles and nearly black spots.

Horn sharks inhabit rocky areas, often in deep crevices and caves, kelp beds, sandy gullies, and flats. The juveniles often shelter on sandy bottoms. They are nocturnal, seldom moving from their preferred resting place by day. They are poor, sluggish swimmers, so their home ranges are small. It is thought that there is a limited winter migration into deep water in the northern part of its range. They crawl over the seabed using their mobile, muscular, paired fins. Usually solitary, some small aggregations have been reported.

Size Egg case: 4–4.5 x 1–1.5 in. Mature: 23–23.5 in. TL ♂, ♀ larger. Max: 48 in. TL.
Distribution East Pacific: U.S. (California), Mexico (Baja California, Gulf of California), probably Ecuador and Peru.
Food Benthic invertebrates and, rarely, small fish.
Breeding Eggs deposited February–April, hatch in seven–nine months.
Status Least concern. Minimal fisheries interest. Caught by divers for sport; may bite when provoked.

Zebra Bullhead Shark *Heterodontus zebra*

This bullhead shark is unmistakable. Its background color is white or cream, and over this is a striking, zebra-striped pattern of numerous black or dark brown vertical saddles and bands over the body, tail, and head. In juveniles, these bands are red brown.

Little is known about this species. It is found on continental and insular shelves of the western Pacific and in the South China Sea. It is found in deeper water off western Australia.

Size ♂'s immature at 17 in., mature at 25 in. Max: 48 in. TL.
Distribution Western Pacific: Japan, Koreas, China, Taiwan Island, Vietnam, Indonesia, northwestern Australia.
Food Not known.
Breeding Not known.
Status Least concern. Apparently it is common and taken in bycatch.

CARPETSHARKS

This order (Orectolobiformes) contains about 33 species in seven families:

> Collared carpetsharks (Parascylliidae)—7 species
> Blind sharks (Brachaeluridae)—2 species
> Wobbegongs (Orectolobidae)—7 species
> Longtailed carpetsharks (Hemiscylliidae)—12 species
> Nurse sharks (Ginglymostomatidae)—3 species
> Zebra Shark (Stegostomatidae)—1 species
> Whale Shark (Rhincodontidae)—1 species

They range from the small, like the 14-in. long collared carpetsharks, to the gigantic Whale Shark with reports of nearly 69 ft. Virtually all are bottom living, and many are strikingly marked, some with very complex patterns. All have two spineless dorsal fins and an anal fin. Their nostrils have barbels, which are rudimentary in the Whale Shark, and are connected via the nasoral grooves to the short mouth that ends in front of the eyes.

They are found worldwide in warm temperate and tropical seas, from the intertidal zone to deep water. They have the greatest diversity and endemism in the tropical Indo-west Pacific. The smallest species are mainly sluggish and bottom living. However, the larger species tend to be more active and wide ranging. This seen especially in the circumglobal pelagic Whale Shark.

They utilize a variety of reproductive strategies, including egg-laying (oviparity), or the fetuses are retained inside the female and nourished by their yolk sacs until birth (ovoviviparity or aplacental viviparity), or egg-eating (oophagy).

Closeup view of a Necklace Carpetshark (above) and a Cobbler Wobbegong (below), showing the different types of barbels associated with the nostrils.

Collared Carpetsharks

This family consists of two genera in the west Pacific. All four *Parascyllium* species are Australian endemics, and in *Cirrhoscyllium* the three species occur from Vietnam to Japan. They are small slender sharks with their mouths entirely in front of the eyes, and tiny spiracles. *Cirrhoscyllium* have unique cartilage-cored paired barbels on the throat, dark saddles and no spots or collar markings. *Parascyllium*, on the other hand, have no throat barbels, but do have saddles and spots.

Some species are hardy in captivity. They may be taken in bycatch and therefore be threatened in heavily fished areas.

Barbelthroat Carpetshark
Cirrhoscyllium expolitum

It has six to ten diffuse saddle marks on the back, and an elongated rounded saddle on each side of the back and tail, between the pectoral and pelvic fins bases, which extends over the pelvic fin bases. The paired throat barbels are have a core of cartilage.

Little is known about this benthic species, which may be able to change color to match the seabed. They are found on the outer continental shelf.

Size Known from two females, 12 in. and (adult) 13 in. TL.
Distribution South China Sea, northwestern Pacific between China and the Philippines and near Vietnam (Gulf of Tonkin).
Food Not known.
Breeding Presumed oviparous.
Status Not evaluated. Presumably rare or uncommon, taken as bycatch.

Necklace Carpetshark *Parascyllium variolatum*

A dark grayish to chocolate-brown small shark with an unmistakable, highly variable pattern. It has a broad, dark, white-spotted collar over the gill region and obvious black spots on all fins. The body has dark blotches with scattered white dots and lines of dense white spots. Another white-spotted form has recently been found in Western Australia, which may be an undescribed species.

It lives in a variety of habitats on the continental shelf, including sand, rocky reefs, kelp, and seagrass beds. It is nocturnal. The juveniles hide under rocks and bottom debris in shallow water.

Size Max: ~35 in. TL.
Distribution Southern Australia. (Eastern and western forms may be more than one species.)
Food Not known.
Breeding Virtually unknown, probably oviparous. Like other collared carpetsharks they are thought to lay elongated flattened egg cases.
Status Least concern. Not targeted by fisheries, rare in bycatch.

Blind Sharks

Named because they close their eyelids when out of water. Endemic to eastern Australian coast. There are two mono-specific genera, *Brachaelurus* and *Heteroscyllium*.

Small, stout sharks with two spineless dorsal fins set far back. They have large spiracles below and behind the eyes, nasoral and circumnarial grooves, and long barbels.

Ovoviviparous (litters of six to eight finish absorbing their large yolksacs just before birth). Blind sharks feed on small fish, crustaceans, squid, and sea anemones.

Both have very restricted geographic range.

Bluegray Carpetshark
Heteroscyllium cocloughi

Adult is grayish above and white below. The young have conspicuous black markings on the back, dorsal fins, and caudal fin, which fade in adults. It has a pair of long barbels with posterior hooked flaps.

Lives inshore, on the bottom, in less than 20 ft. depth.

Size Mature ~19.5 in. ♂, 25.5 in. ♀. Max: >29.5 in. TL.
Distribution Eastern Australia.
Food Not known.
Breeding Aplacentally viviparous, six–eight pups/litter.
Status Vulnerable. Known from about 20 specimens in a small, well surveyed area heavily used by fisheries and for recreation. Presumed rare.

Blind Shark *Brachaelurus waddi*

This brown, small, stout shark has scattered white spots and a light yellowish underneath. The young have dark saddles, which normally fade in adults. The similar-sized dorsal fins are set far back with the origin of the first over the pelvic fin bases. The second dorsal is well in front of the anal fin origin, with the anal and lower caudal fins almost touching. It has a large spiracle, nasoral and circumnarial grooves, long tapering barbels, and a small mouth in front of the eyes.

It is usually found on rocky shores (tidepools), reefs, seagrass beds, from the shallows down to 459 ft. The juveniles often occur in high-energy surge zones.

Blind Sharks are nocturnal, hiding in caves and under ledges by day and coming out at night to feed. They can survive long periods of time out of the water.

Size Mature: <23.5 in. ♂, <26 in. ♀. Max: 47 in. TL.
Distribution Eastern Australia.
Food Small fish, crustaceans, squid, and sea anemones.
Breeding Seven–eight pups/litter in November.
Status Least concern. Relatively common. Collected for aquaria. Rarely taken in fisheries. Extremely hardy and survives release well.

Wobbegongs

This family contains three genera with seven species. They live on the bottom in warm temperate to tropical continental waters, from the intertidal zone to greater than 360 ft. deep, often on rocks and coral reefs or on sandy bottoms.

They are very distinctive, flattened, highly patterned, well camouflaged sharks. There are dermal flaps along the sides of their broad, flat heads. They have long barbels and short mouths in front of the eyes, almost at the very front of the short snout. The jaws are heavy with two rows of enlarged, sharp, fanglike teeth in the upper jaw and three in the lower. They have a complex nasal and oral area with nasoral grooves, circumnarial grooves and flaps, and symphysial grooves. Their spiracles are larger than their upward-facing eyes. They have two spineless dorsal fins and an anal fin. The first dorsal fin's origin is over the pelvic fin bases.

All are ovoviviparous with large litters of 20 or more. They are powerful seabed predators on bottom-living animals such as fish, crabs, lobsters, and octopi. They hide camouflaged by their patterned skin and dermal lobes around the head, sucking in and impaling prey on their large teeth. They clamber around the bottom using their paired fins and even do so out of the water.

They are potentially dangerous and bite if provoked. Some species are kept and bred in aquaria. Some are important in fisheries.

Tasselled Wobbegong
Eucrossorhinus dasypogon

This wobbegong has a complex reticulated pattern of narrow, dark lines on a light background, with scattered, symmetrical, enlarged dark dots at the line junctions, and indistinct saddles. It has many highly branched dermal lobes on the head and a "beard" on the chin. The paired fins are very broad.

Found in inshore coral reefs, especially around coral heads, channels, and reef faces. It is nocturnal and possibly solitary with a small home range. By day it rests, with its tail curled, on the bottom in caves and under ledges.

Size Mature: <46 in. ♂. Max: >49 in. TL.
Distribution Southwestern Pacific: Indonesia (Wai-geo, Aru), New Guinea, Australia. (Malaysia?)
Food Bottom fish, possibly invertebrates. Catches nocturnal fish sharing its caves.
Breeding Presumably ovoviviparous.

Status Near threatened. Reef destruction and fisheries a threat in much of range (least concern in Australia). Reported to bite divers.

Japanese Wobbegong *Orectolobus japonicus*

This wobbegong has a very obvious color pattern of broad, dark dorsal saddles with spots and blotches. These saddles have dark, but not black, corrugated edges separated by lighter areas, with dark, broad reticular lines. There are five dermal lobes below and in front of the eyes and on each side of the head. The nasal barbels are long and branched.

Occurs in tropical inshore rocky and coral reefs, but rarely seen by divers because of their nocturnal lifestyle.

Size Mature: <40 in. ♀. Max: >42 in. TL.
Distribution Northwestern Pacific: Japan, Korea, China, Taiwan Island, Vietnam.
Food Benthic fish, also skate, shark egg cases, cephalopods, and shrimp.
Breeding Ovoviviparous, up to 20–23 pups/litter born in spring (March–May) in captivity in Japan. One year gestation.
Status Not evaluated.

Cobbler Wobbegong *Sutorectus tentaculatus*

This strikingly patterned and distinctive wobbegong has broad, dark dorsal saddles with jagged, corrugated edges. These saddles are separated by light areas with irregular dark spots. This wobbegong is somewhat slender, less flattened than most wobbegongs, with a rather narrow head. The chin is smooth with only a few slender, short, unbranched dermal lobes on the sides of the head. These form isolated groups of lobes broadly separated from one another, in four to six pairs. They have simple, long, unbranched nasal barbels. There are distinctive rows of large, warty dermal tubercles on the back and bases of the very low, long dorsal fins, the height of which is half the base length.

Cobbler Wobbegongs are found around rocky and coral reefs and also in seaweeds. As yet their depth has not been recorded. Not much else is known about this species.

Size Mature: ~25.5 in. ♂. Max: recorded 36 in. TL.
Distribution Southern and western Australia.
Food Not known.
Breeding Not known.
Status Least concern. Common, bycatch usually returned alive.

Longtailed Carpetsharks

There are two genera occurring in the Indo-west Pacific; *Chiloscyllium*, with seven wide-ranging species, and *Hemiscyllium*, with five, possibly six species, mainly in the western Pacific and also Seychelles. They occur in intertidal pools, very shallow water, rocky and coral reefs close inshore, and on sediments in inshore and offshore in bays.

They are small, mostly less than 3 ft. in length, and slender, with very long tails. They have two equal-sized, unspined dorsal fins; the origin of the second is well ahead of the long, low rounded anal fin, which is separated by a notch from the lower caudal fin. Their small transverse mouth is well in front of the dorsolateral eyes with large spiracles below them. They have nasoral and circumnarial grooves and short barbels. The color patterns of the young are often different and bolder than the adults. *Chiloscyllium* species are without a black hood on the head or large dark spots on the sides of the body, with the mouth closer to the eyes than the snout tip. *Hemiscyllium* species have spots or a hood, with nostrils at the end of the snout, and obvious ridges above the eyes.

Their biology is poorly known. Some, presumably all, are oviparous, laying oval egg cases. The distinct color patterns of the young suggest different habitat preferences from the adults. Strong, muscular, leglike paired fins are used to clamber on reefs and in crevices. The large epaulette spots on *Hemiscyllium* species may be eyespots to intimidate predators. Their food includes small bottom fish, cephalopods, shelled mollusks, and crustaceans.

They are taken in multispecies fisheries and as bycatch, sometimes in large numbers. They are hardy, attractive, and bred in captivity. Often common to abundant, but some species are rare, with limited distribution in threatened habitats.

Whitespotted Bambooshark
Chyloscyllium plagiosum

Dark body, with numerous light and dark spots, dark bands, and saddles, which are not conspicuously edged with black. The dorsal fins, which have straight or convex rear margins, and anal fin are set far back on the very long thick tail — so far back that the first dorsal fin origin is opposite or just behind the pelvic fin insertions. There are lateral ridges running along the trunk.

Whitespotted Bamboosharks occur inshore on the bottom of reefs in the tropics. Being nocturnal, they rest in reef crevices by day and come out to feed at night.

Size Mature: ~19.5–23.5 in. ♂. Max: 37 in. TL.
Distribution Indo-west Pacific: Madagascar to Indonesia, Philippines and Japan.
Food Bony fish and crustaceans.
Breeding Oviparous.
Status Near threatened. Common and important in inshore fisheries. Used for food. Popular aquarium species.

Epaulette Shark *Hemiscyllium ocellatum*

This species gets its name from the large, dark spot on its "shoulder" (an epaulette is an ornament worn on the shoulder of a uniform). The dorsal and anal fins are set far back on the long thick tail. There are no spots on the snout, but there are dark spots on the body and unpaired fins, which are much smaller than the conspicuous large black epaulette spot. This is ringed with white, and has inconspicuous small dark spots behind and below. It has no white spots or reticular network. The pale-margined, dark, paired fins found in the young fade in the adults. There are sometimes a few small dark spots on the adult paired fins. Dark bands occur around the tails of the young, the adults having no bands and a uniform light ventral tail surface.

Live in coral niches, particularly staghorn, in shallow water and tidepools, sometimes barely submerged. Usually nocturnal, and often feeds at low tide. It crawls, clambers, and swims around. When digging in the sand their tail thrashes around. Seems unafraid of man, but may nip when captured.

Size Mature: 23–24 in. ♂, ~25 in. ♀. Max: 42 in. TL.
Distribution Southwestern Pacific: New Guinea and Australia (possibly to Solomon Islands and Malaysia).
Food Worms, crustaceans, and small fish.
Breeding Oviparous, eggs hatch in about 120 days.
Status Least concern. Abundant on the Great Barrier Reef; may be threatened in New Guinea.

Hooded Carpetshark *Hemiscyllium strahani*

Like the Epaulette, the dorsal and anal fins are set far back on the extremely long, thick tail. What is distinctive is the black, or very dark, mask on the adult snout and head. Black spots and bands also occur beneath the head but not on the snout. Its black epaulette spot is partially merged with the shoulder saddle and is not quite surrounded by a white ring. It has dark saddles and blotches on the body, with many white spots on the body and fins, however, there is no reticular pattern. The margins of the paired fins are white-spotted on black, and there are dark rings around the tail.

Hooded Carpetsharks live inshore on coral reef faces and flats. Nocturnal, like the Epaulette, they hide in crevices and under table corals by day.

Size Mature: before 23 in. ♂, 29 in. ♀. Max: 31 in. TL.
Distribution Eastern Papua New Guinea.
Food Not known.
Breeding Not known.
Status Vulnerable. Small, fragmented range is polluted and fished using dynamite.

Nurse Sharks

This group contains three monospecific genera of subtropical and tropical sharks. They occur in continental and insular waters, including coral and rocky reefs, sandy areas, reef lagoons, and mangrove keys. They occur in intertidal and surf zones, sometimes barely covered, to at least 230 ft.

Their mouths are transverse and subterminal. There are long nasoral grooves in front of the eyes. The nostrils have barbels. The spiracles are small, as are the gill slits, with the 5th almost overlapping the 4th. The second dorsal fin is level with, and about same size as, the anal fin; the latter is close to the lower caudal fin. Their caudal fins are elongated with a strong terminal lobe, but with no, or a very short, ventral lobe.

All are nocturnal and social, resting on the bottom, by day, in small groups. They cruise near, or clamber on the bottom, with their mouths and barbels close to the substrate, searching for food. With their small mouths and large pharynx cavities they can suck in, like a vacuum cleaner, a variety of bottom-living invertebrates and fish, including active reef fish.

The larger species are, or were, formerly common and often caught in local inshore fisheries for food, liver oil, and their tough leather. Not usually aggressive, they can bite hard and hang on tight if provoked.

Nurse Shark *Ginglymostoma cirratum*

The Nurse Shark's dorsal fins are broadly rounded, the first is much larger than the second and anal fin. Adults are uniform yellow- to gray-brown. The young have small, dark, light-ringed ocellar spots and obscure saddle markings.

Nurse Sharks occur on rocky and coral reefs, and in channels between mangrove keys and sand flats on tropical and subtropical continental and insular shelves. They rest in groups, even piles, by day in preferred shallow-water locations on sand or in caves. They are strong swimmers and are active at night. Often they use their muscular pectoral fins to clamber on the bottom, and their snout to root out prey. Their courtship and mating behavior includes synchronized swimming, with their sides nearly touching, the male beside or slightly behind and below the female. The male then bites one of the female's pectoral fins and both roll upside-down on the seabed to mate.

Size Mature: ~82.5 in. ♂, 90.5–94.5 in. ♀. Max: ~118+ in. TL.
Distribution East Pacific: Mexico to Peru. West Atlantic: U.S. to Gulf, Caribbean, and Brazil. Eastern Atlantic: Cape Verde Islands, Senegal, Cameroon to Gabon (rarely north to France).
Food Bottom invertebrates, bony fish, and stingrays. Can extract conch snails from intact shell.
Breeding Ovoviviparous: 20–30 pups/litter with large yolk-sacs. Females reproduce every other year. Juvenile nursery areas in shallow turtle-grass beds and coral reefs.
Status Data deficient. Historically common in many areas, but small home ranges and aggregating habits make it highly vulnerable to local extirpation. Docile, popular with divers, and hardy in aquaria, but will bite if provoked.

Tawny Nurse Shark *Nebrius ferrugineus*

These sharks have fairly long barbels and tiny spiracles. The large first dorsal fin base is over the pelvic fin bases. The dorsal, pectoral, and anal fins are angular with sharpish tips. Their color may change between shades of brown, depending on habitat.

They occur on or near the bottom in sheltered areas. Usually they are nocturnal and prowl the reefs by night searching for prey to suck out of crevices. They aggregate in shelter by day. They often return to the same resting place. Known to "spit" water when caught and spin on the line when hooked.

Size Mature: ~98 in. Max: 123.5–126 in. TL.
Distribution Wide ranging, tropical Indo-Pacific: South Africa to Red Sea and Gulf, Eastern Asia north to Japan, Australia to Marshall Islands and Tahiti.
Food Corals, crustaceans, cephalopods, sea urchins, and reef fish, occasionally sea snakes.
Breeding Ovoviviparous. Young feed inside the uterus on large, infertile, yolky eggs (oophagy). Litter size uncertain (one–four, depending on competition in the uterus).
Status Vulnerable. Fished through much of its range. Local extirpations reported. Small litters and limited dispersion will prevent rapid recovery from overfishing. Docile and popular with divers, may bite if harassed.

Shorttail Nurse Shark
Pseudoginglymostoma brevicaudatum

Small, dark brown nurse shark with no spots or markings. The color of the young is unknown. It is distinguished from all other nurse sharks by its short nasal barbels and short precaudal tail and caudal fin, which is less than 20% of its total length. It also has equal-sized, rounded dorsal and anal fins.

These sharks occur in and around coral reefs but to what depths is not known, or recorded. They have been found to be nocturnal in captivity, but otherwise their biology is poorly known. There have been reports that they are able to survive for several hours out of the water.

Size Mature: ~21.5–22 in. ♀. Max: 29.5 in. TL. Adult ♀, 33 years in captivity, is 27.5 in. long.
Distribution Western Indian Ocean: Tanzania, Kenya, and Madagascar, possibly Mauritius and Seychelles.
Food Not known.
Breeding Presumed oviparous (egg-laying observed in captivity).
Status Vulnerable. Its coral reef habitat is heavily fished and damaged in many areas.

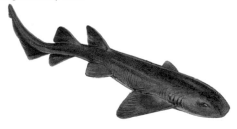

Zebra Shark

Unmistakable shark at all ages. The juveniles are dark brown above, yellowish below, with vertical yellow stripes and spots separating dark saddles. These break up into small brown spots on yellow in intermediate sharks 19.5 to 35.5 in. long. The larger the shark, the more uniformly they are distributed over the body. The broad caudal fin is as long as the body. The mouth is small and transverse and positioned in front of the lateral eyes. They have small barbels and large spiracles. The first dorsal fin is set forward on the back and is much larger than the second. Its anal fin is close to the tail.

It lives on coral reefs and offshore sediments, from intertidal areas to 200 ft. deep. The adults and large spotted juveniles rest in coral reef lagoons, channels, and faces. Striped young are rarely seen and may be found deeper, possibly to more than 165 ft. Their behavior is poorly known. It is thought that they rest propped up on their pectoral fins, mouth open, facing the current. Usually they are solitary, aggregations being rarely seen. They are sluggish by day and more active at night or when food is present. They can swim strongly and are able to squirm into crevices to search for food.

Zebra Shark *Stegostoma fasciatum*

Size Mature: 58–72 in. ♂, 66.5–67 in. ♀. Max: possibly 140 in. TL, mostly <98 in.
Distribution Indo-west Pacific: tropical continental and insular shelves, eastern Africa to Japan, New Caledonia, and Palau.
Food Mollusks, crustaceans, small bony fish, possibly sea snakes.
Breeding Oviparous, lays large dark brown or purplish-black egg cases, anchored to bottom with fine tufts of fibers.
Status Vulnerable. Relatively common, but taken in many fisheries, and its coral reef habitat is threatened. Not aggressive. Kept in captivity.

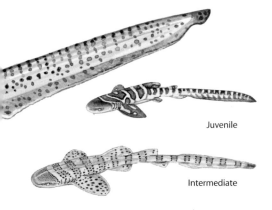

Juvenile

Intermediate

Whale Shark

This shark is an unmistakable, huge filter-feeder with a checkerboard pattern of yellow or white spots on gray, bluish, or greenish-brown back and white or yellowish underside. The head is broad and flat, with a short snout and huge transverse mouth, which is in front of the eyes and almost terminal. The body has prominent ridges, the lowest of which ends in a keel on the caudal peduncle. The large caudal fin is lunate and unnotched.

They are pelagic, found from the open ocean to close inshore off beaches, coral reefs, and islands, from the surface to more than 2,300 ft. Location of pupping and nursery grounds are unknown. They migrate long distances. Tagging and photo-identification indicate that they are regular visitors to favored feeding sites at annual, seasonal, or lunar fish and invertebrate spawning events. The high density of plankton produced on these occasions is consumed by suction feeding and gulping, often while hanging vertically. Their long-distance, long-term migrations include one of 8,080 miles (in one direction only) over 37 months.

Whale Shark *Rhincodon typus*

Size Mature: >225 in. ♂, >315 in. ♀. Max: possibly 670–830 in. TL.

Distribution Circumglobal, all tropical and warm temperate seas except Mediterranean.

Food Planktonic crustaceans and fish eggs.

Breeding Ovoviviparous. One female from Taiwan had about 300 pups in her uterus.

Status Vulnerable. Has been fished for meat, apparently unsustainably, in many areas. Steep declines in yields reported from the Philippines, Taiwan, Maldives, and India. Legally protected in many states. Listed on Appendix II of CITES (to ensure that international trade is sustainable) and Appendix II of the Convention on Migratory Species (to encourage international collaborative management).

MACKEREL SHARKS

The mackerel sharks (Lamniformes) consist of seven families and 15 species of mainly large, active pelagic sharks.

They have cylindrical bodies, two spineless dorsal fins, the first originating over the abdomen, well in front of the pelvic fin origins and anal fin. Their vertebral axis extends into a long upper tail lobe. The head is conical with a fairly short snout and five broad gill openings—the hind two are in front or above the pectoral fin origins. The mouth is large, extending behind the eyes, and free from the nostrils, with no barbels or grooves. Their spiracles are very small and found well behind the eyes.

They are found worldwide, mostly in warm waters (however, some prefer cold), in a wide range of marine habitats, from the intertidal zones to at least 5,250 ft. deep and also in the open ocean. None occur in fresh water. Behavior is also very varied, from slow coastal sharks to fast oceanic swimmers, top predators to carrion and filter feeders. Some mackerel sharks are highly migratory. Many others are social and some will even hunt cooperatively. Reproduction is ovoviviparous (aplacental viviparous); the young eat the eggs in the uterus and at least one species also cannibalizes other embryos. Their diet is varied, anything from marine mammals, birds, and reptiles to other sharks, rays, bony fish, and invertebrates.

Several species are very important in coastal commercial and sport fisheries and highly valued for their sport, flesh, and fins. Others are rare and not often recorded. A few of the larger species occasionally bite people, but are also important for dive ecotourism and moviemakers. Only one species is commonly kept in aquaria. Most are under threat from overfishing and others are completely unmonitored.

Crocodile Shark *Pseudocarcharias kamoharai*

This small mackerel shark has a gray or gray-brown back and lighter underside, with light-edged fins. It is a very distinctive, slender-bodied oceanic shark with small fins, huge eyes, long gill slits, and prominent long slender teeth on highly protrusable jaws.

They are usually found well offshore, far from land, and found from the surface to at least 1,935 ft. It is probably a strong active swimmer. It may migrate vertically to the surface at night, and to deeper water by day.

Size Born: 16 in. TL. Mature: ~29 in. ♂, 35–43 in. ♀. Max: 43 in. TL.
Distribution Worldwide, oceanic tropical waters.
Food Not known.
Breeding Ovoviviparous, four pups/litter feed on unfertilized eggs and possibly cannibalize other young before birth.
Status Near threatened. Population depletion very likely as a result of bycatch in pelagic longline fisheries, although they are not commercially valuable.

Sandtiger Sharks

These are large heavy-bodied sharks with pointed snouts with upper precaudal pits, but no lower pits. The caudal fin is asymmetrical and without keels. There are three species.

Size Mature: ~86 in. Max: >170 in. TL.
Distribution Warm-temperate and tropical Atlantic, Mediterranean, and Indo-west Pacific. (Not central and eastern Pacific.)
Food Wide range of fish and invertebrates.
Breeding Two young born every other year, one from each uterus. Each surviving embryo kills and eats smaller embryos and feeds on unfertilized eggs during 9–12 month pregnancy. One unborn pup bit an investigating scientist.
Status Vulnerable. Many populations seriously depleted. Critically endangered in NSW, Australia, after large numbers were killed in sports and commercial fisheries and by divers. Legally protected in many countries. Docile and has bred in captivity. Important for dive ecotourism in South Africa and Australia. May bite if approached too closely.

Sandtiger Shark *Carcharias taurus*

A large, heavy, light brown shark, often with scattered darker spots. The conical snout is flattened and the long mouth extends behind the eyes, with large slender pointed teeth. The long gill openings are in front of the pectoral fins. Its large dorsal and anal fins are similar in size; the first dorsal is closer to the pelvic than to the pectoral fins. The tail is asymmetrical with a short lower lobe.

It is found in coastal waters, from the surf zone to offshore reefs. It is associated with underwater caves, gullies, and reefs. Usually on or near the bottom, and occasionally midwater or surface. It is a slow but strong swimmer and more active at night. Air is swallowed at the surface and held in the stomach to provide neutral buoyancy, enabling the shark to hover in the water. They have complex social, courtship, and mating behavior, which has been studied in captivity and the wild. They may aggregate in schools of 20 to 80 for feeding (they have been observed to herd prey fishes), courtship, mating, and birth. Some are highly migratory, moving to cooler water in summer.

Smalltooth Sandtiger *Odontaspis ferox*

This shark differs from the Sandtiger by its long conical snout, fairly large eyes, the first dorsal fin being closer to the pectoral fin bases than pelvics and larger second dorsal and anal fins. It is gray or gray-brown above and lighter below, often with darker spots.

Smalltooth Sandtigers occur on or near the bottom of continental and insular shelves and upper slopes. They are possibly epipelagic in depths of 460 to 590 ft. Sometimes they are seen near coral reef dropoffs, rocky reefs, and gullies. They are active offshore swimmers, reportedly solitary or in small groups near reefs and gullies.

Size Mature: 108 in. ♂, 143 in. ♀. Max: >160 in. TL.
Distribution May be worldwide in warm temperate and tropical deep water.
Food Small bony fish, squid, and shrimp.
Breeding Reproduction poorly known.
Presumed viviparous, pups nourished by
oophagy. Litter size unknown.
Status Vulnerable in Australia.
Rare and declining.

Bigeye Sandtiger *Odontaspis noronhai*

This sandtiger shark differs to the other sandtigers by its uniform, unspotted, dark reddish-brown to black coloration. It has the largest eyes of all sandtigers, which are blue to blue green. The first dorsal fin is larger than the second dorsal and anal fins, and often has a white blotch on the tip.

It usually inhabits the midwater in the open ocean, or near the bottom on continental and island slopes. The uniform dark color also suggests this is an oceanic midwater species. Its behavior is poorly known. Probably migrates vertically in midocean, near the surface at night and into deep water by day.

Size Mature: >86.5 in. ♂, ~128 in. ♀. Max: at least 142 in. TL.
Distribution Known from a few confirmed records in Atlantic and Central Pacific. May be worldwide in deep warm seas.
Food Not known.
Breeding Not known.
Status Data deficient.

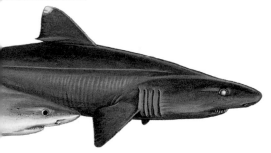

Goblin Shark

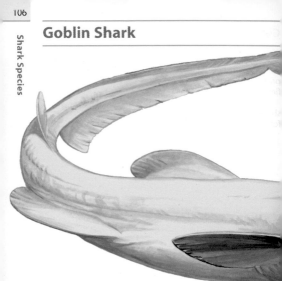

Size Mature: <104 in. ♂, <132 in. ♀. Max: 151 in. TL.
Distribution Atlantic, western Indian Ocean, and Pacific.
Patchy distribution.
Food Slender front teeth suggest a diet of small, soft-bodied
fish and squid, but back teeth are modified to crush food.
Breeding Not known.
Status Least concern. Widely distributed in very deep water.
Occasionally bycatch in deepwater fisheries.

Goblin Shark *Mitsukurina owstoni*

This bizarre shark has a soft, flabby, pinkish-white body. The elongated, flat, bladelike snout is unique to this shark. It has protrusible jaws with long-cusped slender teeth. The caudal fin is long, with no ventral lobe.

This is a deepwater shark inhabiting the outer continental shelves and upper slopes and off seamounts. It is very rarely found at the surface.

Its body form suggests it is a poor swimmer. The bladelike snout may be used to locate prey using sensors on the underside to detect the electrical fields produced by muscular activity of their prey. Its highly specialized jaws can shoot forward rapidly to snap up prey. Not much else is known about this shark.

Megamouth Shark

Megamouth Shark *Megachasma pelagios*

This shark was only discovered during the last thirty years, despite its size. It is the smallest of the shark plankton feeders, but is still a giant reaching more than 18 ft. in total length. It is gray above and white below with dark spotting on the lower jaw. The pectoral and pelvic fins are blackish with light rear margins. It has an unmistakable, large, long head with a short rounded snout. The huge terminal mouth extends behind the eyes and has numerous small hooked teeth.

It is oceanic, coastal, and found offshore. It probably migrates vertically with the plankton and is close to the surface at night, but deeper by day. It is thought to have luminescent tissue inside its mouth to attract prey. There is still much more we need to find out about this shark and only recently have live specimens been filmed.

Size Mature: ~157 in. ♂, ~197 in. ♀. Max: >216.5 in. TL.
Distribution Probably worldwide in the tropics (not many records).
Food Plankton, particularly shrimp, possibly by suction.
Breeding Reproduction unknown, presumed viviparous with oophagy.
Status Data deficient. Very rarely recorded.

Thresher Sharks

There are three species of large-eyed sharks in this family, all belonging to one genus. They have small mouths, large pectoral, pelvic, and first dorsal fins, and tiny second dorsal and anal fins. The caudal fin is very elongated, curved, and whiplike. They easily distinguish this group of sharks and are as long as their bodies.

Thresher Shark *Alopias vulpinus*

Large blue-gray to dark gray sharks, with silvery or coppery sides. Their white underside is clearly demarcated from the sides and extends in a patch above the pectoral fins. They also have a white dot on the tip of each narrow, pointed pectoral fin. The upper lobe of the caudal fin is about as long as the rest of the shark. They have fairly large eyes on the side of the head and they also have labial furrows.

Thresher Sharks are found from nearshore to far offshore and from the surface to at least 1,200 ft. deep. They are most abundant near land (pups use inshore nurseries) and in temperate water. They migrate seasonally along the coast and have been seen leaping out of the water.

Size Mature: ~118 in. ♂, 146–157 in. ♀. Max: 228 in. TL.
Distribution Oceanic and coastal, almost worldwide in tropical to cold-temperate seas.
Food Herds and stuns small fishes with its tail, sometimes cooperatively.
Breeding Ovoviviparous, two–six (usually four) pups/litter Feed on infertile eggs (oophagy).
Status Data deficient. Near threatened in Californian waters. Highly vulnerable to fisheries, likely depleted.

Pelagic Thresher *Alopias pelagicus*

These are the smallest threshers. Their bodies are deep blue above and white below with no white above the pectoral fins. The long curving caudal fin has an upper lobe nearly as long as the rest of the shark. The eyes are fairly large, the head very narrow with a straight forehead and an arched profile and no labial furrows. The straight pectoral fins are broad tipped.

They are oceanic, wide-ranging, usually offshore sharks, which are sometimes found nearshore on narrow continental shelves, sometimes near coral reefs, dropoffs, and seamounts. They are poorly known, active, strong swimmers, and are probably migratory. They have been seen repeatedly leaping out of the water.

Size Mature: ~98–118 in. Max: 144 in. TL.
Distribution Indo-Pacific: South Africa to Australia, Tahiti, China, Japan, U.S., Mexico, and Galapagos.
Food Prey unknown, presumably small fish and squid.
Breeding Ovoviviparous, two pups/litter (one from each uterus) feed on unfertilized eggs (oophagy).
Status Not evaluated. Highly vulnerable to oceanic fisheries and likely depleted.

Bigeye Thresher *Alopias superciliosus*

A very distinctive purplish-gray to gray-brown thresher shark with a light gray to white underside, which does not extend above the pectoral fins. It has the typical thresher shark caudal fin, which is nearly as long as the rest of the shark. The huge eyes that extend onto the almost flat-topped head make this shark unique. There are deep horizontal grooves above the gills, which run to above the eyes. It has very long narrow pectoral fins and a large first dorsal.

Bigeye Threshers occur in tropical and temperate seas, close inshore out to the open ocean, from the surface down.

Size Mature: ~118 in. ♂, 118–138 in. ♀. Max: >181 in. TL.
Distribution Worldwide, oceanic, and coastal.
Food Uses its tail to stun the pelagic fish on which it feeds.
Breeding Ovoviviparous, two–four pups/litter.
Status Not evaluated. Highly vulnerable to oceanic fisheries and likely depleted.

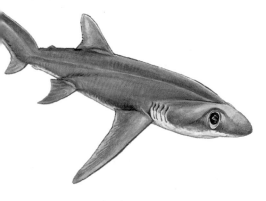

Basking Shark

Size Mature: ~224   in. cm ♂,
800 cm ♀. Max: >395 in. TL.
Distribution Worldwide, cold to warm temperate water.
Food Poorly known plankton-feeder.
Breeding One litter of six pups reported, presumably oophagous.
Status Vulnerable. Endangered regionally, where seriously depleted by target fisheries for oil, meat, and fins. Listed on CITES Appendix II and the Convention on Migratory Species. Protected by several countries and in the Mediterranean.

Basking Shark *Cetorhinus maximus*

Can be seen from coastal vantage points when migrating or feeding inshore. This huge shark is variably colored, usually darker above than below and often with a mottled pattern on the back and sides, with white blotches under the head. This shark is unmistakable with its pointed snout, huge mouth with tiny teeth, and huge gill slits that almost encircle the head. It has strong lateral keels on the caudal peduncle and a lunate caudal fin. Basking Sharks usually occur from the coast to the continental shelf edges and slopes. They are associated with coastal and oceanic fronts. Frequently seen feeding on surface aggregations of plankton, moving slowly forward with their mouths open, sometimes in large groups, of up to 100 or more. They feed on deepwater plankton concentrations in winter. They can leap out of the water. Their huge liver provides buoyancy.

Lamnid Sharks

This group contains five species of large, spindle-shaped sharks with big teeth, conical heads, long gill openings, and crescent-shaped caudal fins with strong caudal keels.

Size Mature: 138–157 in. ♂, 177–197 in. ♀. Max: ~236 in. TL.
Distribution Very wide ranging through most oceans; among the greatest habitat and geographic range of any fish.
Food A wide range of prey, from smaller fish (when young) to large marine mammals when mature.
Breeding Litters of 2–10 pups are nourished by unfertilized eggs during ~12 month gestation at two- to three-year intervals.
Status Vulnerable. Rare, with evidence of depletion through commercial bycatch, beach meshing, and sports fisheries in several parts of the world. Occasionally bites people and jumps into fishing boats. Subject of cage-dive tourism and intensive moviemaking. Protected in several countries. Nominally protected through listing on the Convention on Migratory Species, and international trade regulated through Appendix II of CITES. Not kept successfully in aquaria for long periods.

White Shark *Carcharodon carcharias*

This is a heavy shark with a large first dorsal fin. The second dorsal and anal fins are tiny. It has huge, flat, triangular, serrated teeth and very black eyes. There is a very sharp color change on the flanks from the grayish back to the white underside. There is a black tip underneath the pectoral fins, with usually a black spot where the rear edge joins the body.

White Sharks range widely, from very shallow waters inshore to the open ocean and oceanic islands. They are often seen around rocky reefs near colonies of prey. They are intelligent and inquisitive sharks with highly complex social behavior. Very effective predators, they may breach out of the water when attacking their prey. Satellite and genetic studies indicate that these sharks are highly migratory, crossing ocean basins (i.e. between Mexico and Hawaii, South Africa and Australia). They are warm-blooded, maintaining a constant high body temperature even in cold water.

Longfin Mako *Isurus paucus*

This mako is distinguished from the Shortfin by its less pointed snout, long, relatively broad-tipped pectoral fins (as long as the head), and dusky underside to the snout and mouth in adults.

Widely distributed but very rare, Longfin Makos are possibly epipelagic in deep water in the open ocean. Their behavior is poorly known. They may be a slower swimmer than the Shortfin. Like the Shortfin and the White Shark they are warm blooded.

Size Mature: <96 in. Max: 164 in. TL.
Distribution Oceanic and tropical, probably worldwide (poorly recorded), common in western Atlantic and possibly Central Pacific, rare elsewhere.
Food Fish and squid.
Breeding Litters of two–eight pups (fewer than the Shortfin).
Status Vulnerable. Rare, taken in many fisheries and likely depleted.

Shortfin Mako *Isurus oxyrinchus*

The back of this shark is brilliant blue or purple, with the underside usually white. The front halves of the pelvic fins are dark, the rear and undersides are white. It has a long pointed snout, a "U"-shaped mouth, and large bladelike teeth. The underside of the snout and mouth are white in adults, but dusky in the Azores "marrajo criollo." The pectoral fins are shorter than the head. It has strong keels on the caudal peduncle, with a crescent-shaped caudal fin.

Shortfin Makos are coastal and oceanic, living from the surface to 1,640 ft. in waters warmer than 60°F. They are possibly the fastest shark in the world, highly migratory, and very active, jumping clean out of the water.

Size Mature: ~79–84.5 in. ♂, 108–114 in. ♀. Max: >157.5 in. TL.
Distribution Worldwide in all temperate and tropical seas.
Food Mainly fish and squid, but very large sharks may take small cetaceans.
Breeding Ovoviviparous, 4–25 (mostly 10–18, possibly up to 30) pups/litter feed off unfertilized eggs (oophagy).
Status Near threatened. Taken in bycatch and target fisheries for valuable meat. Some population declines reported. Important "big-game" fish. May attack if provoked. Subject of dive ecotourism.

Porbeagle Shark *Lamna nasus*

Porbeagle Sharks are similar to the Salmon Shark, except for their coloration and distribution. They have a distinctive, white portion of the rear tip dorsal fin that is not attached to the body.

Found in inshore waters to the continental offshore fishing banks, and occasionally the open ocean, from the surface down. They are migratory, moving inshore and to the surface in summer and to offshore deeper waters in winter. Populations are segregated by their age and sex. They are inquisitive and may approach boats and divers but are not dangerous.

Size Mature: 59–79 in. ♂ and 79–98 in. ♀ (smaller in south Pacific). Max: >118 in. TL.
Distribution North Atlantic and cool water (34–64°F) in southern hemisphere, not in equatorial seas or northern Pacific.
Food Small fish, dogfish, Tope, and squid.
Breeding Mostly four pups/litter, feed on unfertilized eggs.
Status Vulnerable. North Atlantic populations endangered by commercial fisheries for high-value meat. Critically endangered in northeastern Atlantic where fisheries are unmanaged. Southern hemisphere status unknown. Also a game fish.

Northern

Southern

Salmon Shark *Lamna ditropis*

This is a heavy bodied, dark gray or blackish shark with dusky blotches on a white underside. The conical snout is dark in adults, with a white patch over the pectoral fin bases. The first dorsal fin has a dark, free rear tip. Like the Porbeagle it has strong keels on its caudal peduncle and a short secondary keel on the base of the crescent-shaped caudal fin.

Salmon Sharks live in cool coastal and oceanic waters, from the surface to at least 740 ft. They are known to be seasonally migratory, following their prey. Segregation within the population is by age and sex, the adults moving farther north than the young. They are able to maintain a constant high body temperature that enables these sharks to actively hunt prey, even in very cold water.

Size Mature: ~71 in. ♂, 86 in. ♀. Max: >118 in. TL.
Distribution Northern Pacific (males common in west, females in east).
Food Schooling fish (salmon, herring, sardines).
Breeding Litters of two–five pups born in spring in nursery grounds.
Status Data deficient. Bycatch in pelagic fisheries largely unrecorded.

GROUND SHARKS

This order (Carcharhiniformes) is the largest, most diverse and widespread group of sharks. It contains about 247 species in eight families:

Catsharks (Scyliorhinidae)—134 species
Finback catsharks (Proscylliidae)—6 species
False catsharks (Pseudotriakidae)—6 species
Barbeled houndsharks (Leptochariidae)—1 species
Houndsharks (Triakidae)—42 species
Weasel sharks (Hemigaleidae)—8 species
Requiem sharks (Carcharhinidae)—53 species
Hammerhead sharks (Sphyrnidae)—7 species

Most are small and harmless to people, but this order also includes some of the largest predatory sharks.

They have a wide range of appearances, from strange bottom-living deepwater sharks, to "typical" large sharks. All have two, spineless dorsal fins and an anal fin. A long mouth extends to or behind the eyes, which are protected by nictitating lower eyelids. If barbels are present, these are developed from anterior nasal flaps of nostrils. The largest teeth are found more on the sides of the mouth, not at the front on either side of symphysis.

They are found worldwide, from cold to tropical seas, intertidal to deep ocean and also pelagic in the open ocean. Some are poor swimmers and are therefore restricted to small areas of the seabed, while others are strong long-distance swimmers and highly migratory.

Ground sharks use very varied reproductive strategies. Many species are oviparous (egg-laying), some deposit eggs on the seabed with the embryos developing for up to a year before hatching, while others retain the eggs until close to hatching. More evolutionarily advanced families retain the fetuses inside the female, nourished either by the yolk sac or by a placenta, until live young are born.

Catsharks

This is by far the largest shark family with at least 134 species in 16 genera, and considerable taxonomic research still needed. More species are continually being discovered and described as commercial fisheries and research efforts move into deeper water. Catsharks are found worldwide, from tropical to arctic waters, usually on or near the seabed, from the intertidal to the deep sea (more than 6,560 ft.), but often restricted to relatively small ranges. Many are rarely seen deepwater species, known from very few specimens (over one-third of *Apristurus* species are known from only one scientifically described specimen and in several cases the original and only specimen has been lost).

Catsharks are usually small, the majority are less than 31.5 in. long, with an elongated body, two small spineless dorsal fins, and an anal fin. They have long arched mouths that reach past the front end of their catlike eyes. Members of some genera, for example the demon catsharks, *Apristurus*, are very difficult to tell apart.

The majority of species are poorly known, particularly the deepwater species. Many of the catsharks lay eggs. The most primitive species lay many pairs of large eggs, protected by tough egg cases with corner tendrils, onto the seabed and hatching may take nearly a year. More advanced species retain their eggs until the embryos' development is almost complete, laying larger numbers of eggs about a month before hatching. A few retain the eggs until the embryos are fully developed and give birth to live young. Some inshore species are nocturnal, sleeping as groups in crevices by day and feeding by night. The majority of species eat benthic invertebrates and small fishes.

None are dangerous to people. A few species are important in fisheries; many are taken as a bycatch and others are regularly kept and breed in aquaria.

Brown Catshark *Apristurus brunneus*

A dark brown demon catshark with obvious light posterior margins on all the fins and the upper caudal fin edge. It has, like most demon catsharks, a broad flattened head with a long snout and large nostrils. The long arched mouth extends to about opposite the front of the green eyes with very long labial furrows, the lower being shorter than the upper. Its gill slits are less than the adult's eye length. The dorsal fins' are equal sized and the first's origin is over the pelvic fins' midbases. It has a small notch between the very large elongated anal fin and the elongated caudal fin.

Brown Catsharks have been found on the outer continental shelf and upper slope, either on or well above the bottom. This is a slightly better known demon catshark but still little is known about its behavior.

Size Eggs: ~5 x 1 in. Mature: 18–19.5 in. ♂, 16.5–19 in. ♀. Max: 27 in. TL.
Distribution Eastern Pacific. Southeastern Alaska to northern Mexico. Possibly Panama, Ecuador, and Peru.
Food Small shrimp, squid, and small fish.
Breeding Oviparous. Pairs of eggs with long tendrils laid in spring and summer (Canada) may take one year to hatch.
Status Data deficient. Bycatch in deepwater fisheries. Probably two species recorded as the Brown Catshark.

Ghost Catshark *Apristurus manis*

This is a dark gray or blackish demon catshark. Its fin tips are sometimes whitish, particularly in juveniles, and there are very few denticles on the side of the body. It has a distinctive stout body, which strongly tapers, wedge-shaped, toward the broad flattened head and elongated snout. Its nostrils are broad with circular apertures. It has a very large, long mouth, much expanded in front of the small, green eyes. The labial furrows are very long, and the gill slits are less than the adult eye length. Underneath they have a distinctive pleated area from behind the mouth to the start of the pectoral fins. The dorsal fins are equal-sized, the first originating over the pelvic fins' midbases. The anal fin is large and broadly rounded, and separated by a small notch from the narrow caudal fin. There is also a crest of enlarged denticles along the uppermost edge of the caudal fin.

Ghost Catsharks occur on continental slopes. Not much else is known about this deepwater catshark.

Size Max: at least 30 in. ♀, 33.5 in. TL (adult ♂).
Distribution Northern and southeastern Atlantic Ocean.
Food Not known.
Breeding Not known.
Status Least concern. Mainly occurs deeper than 3,000 ft. where there is very little fishing.

Orange Spotted Catshark *Asymbolus rubiginosus*

This catshark is pale brown with many dark brown spots on its back and sides. It is named Orange Spotted because these brown spots have orange-brown borders, but there are no spots on the pale underside. It has obscure dark saddles separated by clusters of spots along the spine. Below the eye there is an indistinct brownish blotch and ridge. There is usually a dark mark on the leading and trailing edges of the dorsal fins. The spots on the sides are larger but less distinct. Both dorsal fins are behind the pelvic fins, whose inner margins are fused into an "apron" over the adult male's claspers. The caudal fin is short but broad.

Orange Spotted Catsharks live on the seabed on the continental shelf and upper slope. Little else is known about this species.

Size Adult ♂ 14.5 in. Max: >21 in. TL.
Distribution Eastern Australia, southern Queensland to Tasmania.
Food Not known.
Breeding Thought to lay eggs year round.
Status Least concern. Discarded bycatch in some trawl fisheries.

Gulf Catshark *Asymbolus vincenti*

Another Australian catshark with a mottled grayish-brown or chocolate coloration. It has seven or eight dark saddles and many scattered, small, faint white spots. The underside is pale and unspotted. The head is short and slightly flattened with a short thick snout. Its labial furrows are short and the upper teeth are exposed when the mouth is closed. They have narrow ridges below each eye. The two small dorsal fins are set behind the pelvic fins. As in the Orange Spotted, the inner pelvic fin margins are fused into an "apron" over the adult male's claspers. Its anal fin is short and angular. The caudal fin is short and broad.

These catsharks occur on the seabed. They are found no deeper than 330 ft. in the east, often in seagrass beds. In the Australian Bight, they are found between 425 and 720 ft. deep.

Size Egg case: 5 x $^3/_4$ in. Mature: 15 in ♂. Max: >22 in. TL.
Distribution Southern Australia (most common in Great Australian Bight).
Food Not known.
Breeding Oviparous. Lays pairs of egg cases with long filaments.
Status Least concern. Bycatch in trawl fisheries in only part of its range.

Australian Marbled Catshark
Atelomycterus macleayi

A slender, light gray to gray-brown, narrow-headed catshark with darker gray or brown saddles. These saddles are outlined and partly covered, in adults, by many small black spots, which are also scattered on its sides. It has no white spots and the hatchling young have no spots at all. Their anterior nasal flaps are greatly enlarged and extend right to the mouth. They do have nasoral grooves and the labial furrows are very long. The dorsal fins are set back and much larger than the anal fin; the first dorsal begins above the rear edge of the pelvic fins.

These catsharks occur on and over sand and rock in very shallow water.

Size Egg case: $2^3/_4$ in. Mature: ~19 in. ♂, 20 in. ♀. Max: 23.5 in. TL
Distribution Australia (Western, Northern Territory, possibly Queensland).
Food Not known.
Breeding Oviparous, lays pairs of egg cases.
Status Least concern. Apparently common, no fisheries within its range.

Coral Catshark *Atelomycterus marmoratus*

A dark, narrow-headed slender catshark with no clear saddle markings. It has enlarged black spots that often merge to form dashes and bar marks bridging the saddle areas. There are also scattered large white spots on the sides, back, and fin margins. They have greatly expanded anterior nasal flaps that extend to their long mouth with its nasoral grooves and very long labial furrows. The dorsal fins are much larger than the anal fin. The first dorsal begins opposite or slightly in front of the pelvic fin insertions.

They are to be found, as the name suggests, in crevices and holes on coral reefs. However, little is known about this striking catshark.

Size Mature: 18.5–24 in. ♂, 19–2 in. ♀. Max: 27.5 in. TL.
Distribution Indo-west Pacific: Pakistan and India to New Guinea and southern China.
Food Not known.
Breeding Oviparous, lays pairs of egg cases.
Status Near threatened. Common in artisanal fisheries. Habitat threatened in much of range.

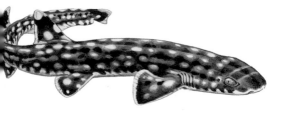

Blackspotted Catshark *Aulohalaelurus labiosus*

This catshark is fairly slender, light grayish to yellowish brown, with a thick-skinned, elongated, cylindrical body. They have a variegated pattern of small to large black spots or blotches, and dark saddles on the sides, back, and fins, with a very few small white spots. The white fin tips are accentuated by dark blotches on the dorsal, caudal, and anal fins. They have a relatively narrow head with a slightly flattened, short, narrowly rounded snout. The dorsal fins are reasonably large and of equal size, the first dorsal begins over or slightly in front of the pectoral fin insertions. Their caudal fin is moderately short but broad.

Found in shallow coastal waters and offshore reefs. Their biology is virtually unknown.

Size Mature: 21–24 in. ♀. Max: 26 in. TL.
Distribution Southwestern Australia.
Food Not known.
Breeding Probably oviparous.
Status Least concern. Common and unfished within range.

Dusky Catshark *Bythaelurus canescens*

A fairly large, plain, dark brown catshark with no markings in the adult, but the young have white fin tips. Their snout is short and rounded and underneath the long, arched mouth reaches to just in front of the large green catlike eyes. There are two small dorsal fins, the first dorsal base is over the pelvic fin bases and the anal fin is almost as large as the second dorsal. The caudal fin is short.

These are deepwater catsharks that occur on mud and rock of the upper continental slope.

Size Adults mature at 23 in. Max: 27.5 in. TL.
Distribution Southeastern Pacific: Peru, Chile, Straits of Magellan.
Food Bottom invertebrates.
Breeding Oviparous, apparently laying pairs of eggs.
Status Not evaluated. Common in deep water, and abundant bycatch in deepwater trawls.

Broadhead Catshark *Bythaelurus clevai*

A distinctive small, gray catshark, which is white below. They have a few large, conspicuous dark brown blotches, saddles, and small spots on the sides and upper surface of the trunk and tail, but the head is nearly plain. The pectoral, pelvic, dorsal, and anal fins all have dark bases and light margins. Their longish snout is narrow and pointed in side view, but broad and bell-shaped from above. The mouth is long and arched, reaching past the front ends of the small catlike eyes. They have two small dorsal fins, the first of which lies mostly over the pelvic fins. Its anal fin is larger than the second dorsal, and high and triangular. The caudal fin is short.

Broadhead Catsharks occur on the upper insular slopes.

Size Mature: ~14–15 in. ♂, 13–15 in. ♀. Max: ~15 in. TL.
Distribution West Indian Ocean, southwestern Madagascar, common off Tulear.
Food Shrimp.
Breeding Ovoviviparous, two pups/litter.
Status Data deficient.

New Zealand Catshark *Bythaelurus dawsoni*

This is a fairly short, light brown or gray-bodied catshark, with a paler, sometimes clearly demarcated, underside. There is a line of white spots on the sides of small animals, and both juveniles and adults have white fin tips. There are also dark bands on the caudal fin. The head is broad and slightly flattened with elongated, lobate anterior nasal flaps. The long, arched mouth reaches past the front end of the large bluish catlike eyes. There are two dorsal fins; the first dorsal is over the pelvic fins, and smaller than the second. The anal fin is short and angular.

These catsharks are found on or near the bottom of the upper slopes of New Zealand and the Auckland Islands.

Size Mature: ~13 in. ♂, 14.5 in. ♀. Max: ~16.5 in. TL.
Distribution New Zealand.
Food Bottom crustaceans.
Breeding Ovoviviparous.
Status Data deficient. Apparently fairly common in deepwater but rarely recorded.

Lollipop Catshark *Cephalurus cephalus*

This is an unmistakable, very small, unpatterned, tadpole-shaped catshark. The rounded head and gill areas are greatly expanded and flattened. The rest of the body and tail is small, slender, very soft, and thin skinned (almost gelatinous). They have two small dorsal fins and an anal fin. The first dorsal fin origin is slightly in front of the pelvic fin origins.

Lollipop Catsharks have been found on or near the bottom of the upper continental slope and outermost shelf. Their expanded gill area suggests that this species is adapted to areas of the seabed with low dissolved oxygen levels. Little else is known about this strange-looking catshark.

Size Born: ~4 in. TL. Mature: ~7.5 in. Max: ~11 in. TL.
Distribution Southern Baja California and Gulf of California, Mexico.
Food Not known.
Breeding Ovoviviparous, retaining its very thin-walled egg cases in the uterus until the two young in the litter hatch.
Status Not evaluated.

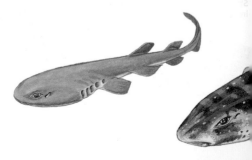

Swellshark *Cephaloscyllium ventriosum*

This is a large, strongly variegated catshark with close-set dark brown saddles and blotches. It has numerous dark spots and occasional light spots on a lighter yellow-brown background and the undersides are also heavily spotted. It has ridges over the eyes. The second dorsal fin is much smaller than the first, and smaller than the anal fin.

Swellsharks occur on rocky bottoms in kelp beds and other algae. They are relatively sluggish and are mainly nocturnal. They can be seen lying motionless in rocky caves and crevices by day, often in small groups, swimming slowly out at night. As their name suggests, they can inflate their stomachs when disturbed to wedge themselves into crevices.

Size Adult: 32–33 in. ♂. Max: >39 in. TL.
Distribution Eastern Pacific, California to Mexico, and Central Chile.
Food Fish, and probably crustaceans.
Breeding Oviparous. Eggs laid in large, unridged greenish-amber, purse-shaped egg cases, hatch in 7.5–10 months (depending on water temperature).
Status Least concern. Not commercially fished. Kept in aquaria.

Reticulated Swellshark
Cephaloscyllium fasciatum

Small, western Pacific catshark with an inflatable stomach. The adults have a striking pattern of dark lines that form open-centered saddles, loops, reticulations, and spots on a light grayish to yellowish background. The young swellsharks do not have any spots. In adults the underside is also spotted. They have ridges over their eyes. The second dorsal fin is much smaller than the first and slightly smaller than the anal fin.

Found on or near muddy bottoms on uppermost continental slopes. They can expand themselves with air or water in an attempt to frighten predators by appearing larger than they really are.

Size Mature: ~14 in. ♂, 17 in. ♀. Max: >17 in. TL.
Distribution Western Pacific: Vietnam, China (Hainan Island), Philippines (Luzon), northwestern Australia.
Food Not known.
Breeding Oviparous.
Status Data deficient globally. Taken as trawl bycatch. Least concern in Australia where fishing effort is limited.

Australian Swellshark *Cephaloscyllium laticeps*

This swellshark has a strongly variegated pattern of dark brown or grayish, close-set, dark saddles and blotches on a lighter gray or chestnut background. Over this pattern there are many dark spots and occasional light spots. There is a broad dark stripe between the eye and the pectoral fin origin; it is also dark below the eye. Its underside is cream, usually with dark stripes down the belly in adults. They have no conspicuous light fin margins. The eyes have ridges over them. The larger first dorsal fin is over the pelvic fin bases and the second is over the anal fin.

They occur inshore on the continental shelf. They have an inflatable stomach presumably used as a predator deterrent.

Size Mature: ~32 in. ♂. Max: >39 in. TL.
Distribution Southern Australia.
Food Small reef fish, crustaceans, and squid.
Breeding Lays ridged cream-colored egg cases attached to seaweed and benthic invertebrates.
Status Least concern. Discarded bycatch from shark gill net fishery; survives well when returned to the sea.

Roughtail Catshark *Galeus arae*

A very small catshark with a striking variegated pattern of dark brown saddle and flank blotches and dark bands on the tail. The saddles and blotches are usually outlined in an off-white color. The dorsal and caudal fin tips are white. As in all *Galeus* species, there is a crest of enlarged dermal denticles along the upper margins of the caudal fin. The mouth has a dark lining.

They are found on or near the bottom of the upper continental and insular slopes. They are partly segregated by depth; only the adults occur in deep water, both adults and juveniles are found above 1,500 ft. They may school in large numbers. Recently this species has been split into three species, the other two are the Antilles and the Longfin Sawtail Catsharks.

Size Mature: ~10.5–13 in. Max: ~13 in. TL.
Distribution Western Atlantic (including Gulf of Mexico and continental Caribbean Sea): two separate populations, one off U.S. (North Carolina to the Mississippi Delta), Mexico, and Cuba, second off Belize, Honduras, Nicaragua, Costa Rica, and adjacent islands.
Food Mainly deepwater shrimp.
Breeding Possibly ovoviviparous.
Status Not evaluated. Common to abundant where it occurs.

African Sawtail Catshark *Galeus polli*

This a fairly small sawtail catshark, with usually about eleven, or fewer, well defined dark gray or blackish-gray saddle blotches. The blotches have a whitish outline on the back and tail and are sometimes uniform dark above. The dorsal and caudal fin tips are pale to white. Like the Roughtail and Blackmouth, their mouth lining is dark. They have a distinct crest of enlarged dermal denticles along the upper margin of the caudal fin, which can easily be felt if handled.

Probably found near the bottom of the upper continental slope and outer continental shelf.

Size Mature 11–18 in. ♂, 12–17 in. ♀. Max: 18 in. TL.
Distribution Eastern Atlantic: southern Morocco to South Africa (west coast).
Food Small fish, squid, and shrimp.
Breeding Ovoviviparous, 6–12 pups/litter.
Status Least concern. Abundant off Namibia. Only the shallow part of its range is heavily fished, and this catshark is small enough to escape from trawls.

Blackmouth Catshark *Galeus melastomus*

A large sawtail catshark and easily recognized by its striking pattern of 15 to 18 dark saddles, blotches, and circular spots on the back and the tail. Its mouth cavity is blackish, hence its common and scientific name. All the fins are white-edged. The precaudal tail is compressed and the long anal fin reaches or extends past the lower caudal fin origin. They have the distinct crest of enlarged dermal denticles, along the upper margin of the caudal fin, common to all sawtail catsharks.

They inhabit the outer continental shelves and upper slopes.

Size Mature: 13–17 in. ♂, 15–18 in. ♀. Max: 35.5 in. TL.
Distribution Northeastern Atlantic and Mediterranean Sea: Faroes and Norway, south to Senegal and Azores.
Food Bottom invertebrates (i.e. shrimp, cephalopods) and lanternfishes.
Breeding Oviparous, up to 13 eggs/female.
Status Not evaluated. Common to abundant where it occurs. Taken as bycatch but low commercial value.

Australian Sawtail Catshark *Galeus boardmani*

A relatively large, grayish sawtail catshark with a variegated pattern of dark grayish brown saddles and bars. It has three broad, pale-edged predorsal saddles, with a narrower and less distinct band between each. There is also a band at and between each dorsal fin, and three broad bands post-dorsally. These bands and saddles are sometimes white flecked. The underside is pale. They have a distinct crest of enlarged dermal denticles along the upper margin of the elongated caudal fin and also along the ventral midline of the caudal peduncle.

They occur at or near the bottom of the outer continental shelf and upper slope and may sometimes aggregate by sex.

Size Mature: ~16 in. ♂, 17 in. ♀. Max: 24 in. TL.
Distribution Australia: southeastern Queensland to western Australia.
Food Fish, crustaceans, and cephalopods, otherwise unknown.
Breeding Oviparous.
Status Least concern. Widespread and apparently common.

Blackspotted or Darkspot Catshark
Halaelurus buergeri

A small catshark with a variegated pattern of dusky bands outlined by large black spots on a light background. The snout is pointed, but not upturned like most other catsharks in this genus. The eyes are raised above the head and the gills are on the upper surface of the head above the mouth.

Occurs on the continental shelf. Little is known about this catshark probably because of its small size and no commercial value.

Size Mature: 14 in. ♂, ~15.75 in. ♀. Max: 19 in. TL.
Distribution Northwestern Pacific: Japan, the Koreas, Philippines, China.
Food Not known.
Breeding Oviparous, several egg capsules are retained in the oviduct and not laid until embryos are advanced and close to hatching.
Status Not evaluated. Common offshore, not fished.

Tiger Catshark *Halaelurus natalensis*

Another striking catshark with tigerlike patterning. The background color is yellow brown above and cream below with ten pairs of broad, dark brown bars enclosing lighter reddish areas and no spots. The snout tip is pointed and upturned and the eyes are raised above its broad head. The gills are also on the upper surface of the head and above the mouth.

Tiger Catsharks live on or near the bottom of the continental shelf, from close inshore to 375 ft. deep, but most records are less than 330 ft. They may segregate by size and depth, as offshore trawls mainly take adults.

Size Egg case: ~4 x $\frac{1}{2}$ in. Adult: 14–18 in. ♂, 14.5–19.5 in. ♀. Max: 19.5 in. ♀ TL.
Distribution Southeastern Atlantic and western Indian Ocean: South Africa. KwaZulu-Natal and Mozambique records need confirmation, possibly based on the similar Lined Catshark.
Food Small bony fish, fish offal, and crustaceans, also polychaetes, cephalopods, and small elasmobranchs.
Breeding Oviparous, 6–11 (mostly 6–9) egg cases per oviduct, laid when embryos close to hatching.
Status Data deficient. Common, bycatch in shrimp trawls.

Puffadder Shyshark
Haploblepharus edwardsii

A beautifully patterned shyshark. The background color is pale to dark, or even gray-brown above and white below. It has prominent golden brown or reddish saddles with darker brown margins and many white spots on the saddles or between them, mostly smaller or the same size as the spiracles. Stocky with a broad head and slender body. The nostrils are very large, with greatly expanded anterior nasal flaps that reach the mouth. The gill slits are on the upper sides of body.

Puffadder Shysharks live on or near sandy and rocky bottoms of the continental shelf, and are found closer inshore in the west of their range. They are apparently social, resting in groups in captivity. They curl up with their tail over their eyes when captured, which is how they got their name.

Size Mature: 14.5–23.5 in. ♂, 15–27 in. ♀. Max: 27 in. TL.
Distribution Southeastern Atlantic and western Indian Ocean: South Africa (eastern and western Cape).
Food Small bony fish, fish offal, crustaceans, cephalopods, and polychaetes.
Breeding Oviparous, egg cases laid in pairs (one/oviduct).
Status Near threatened. Caught by surf anglers, discarded from bottom trawls. Kept in aquaria.

Dark Shyshark *Haploblepharus pictus*

This shyshark has dark dorsal saddle markings and tail band without obvious darker edges. There are sparsely scattered large white spots, with the largest usually over the gill slits, mostly larger than the spiracles and mostly absent between the saddles. The head is broad with very large nostrils and greatly expanded anterior nasal flaps that reach the mouth. The gill slits are on the upper sides of its stocky body.

Occurs on the continental shelf, in kelp forests, on rocky inshore reefs, and sandy areas. From close inshore to depths of about 115 ft. Like all shysharks, they curl up with their tail over their eyes when captured.

Size Adults: 16–22 in. ♂, 14–23.5 in. TL ♀. Max: 23.5 in. TL.
Distribution Southeastern Atlantic and southwestern Indian Ocean: central Namibia to South Africa (East London).
Food Bony fish, sea snails, cephalopods, crustaceans, polychaetes, and echinoderms, occasionally algae.
Breeding Oviparous, one egg laid per oviduct, hatch in about 3.5 months in an aquarium.
Status Not evaluated. Common within limited range. Killed by sports anglers, caught in lobster traps.

Whitespotted Catshark *Holohalaelurus punctatus*

A very small yellow-brown to dark brown catshark with the upper surface densely covered in small closely spaced dark brown spots. It sometimes has faint saddles but there are no other types of complex markings on the body. It is whitish below with scattered tiny black dots beneath the very broad head. There are a few white spots scattered on the back and dorsal fin insertions. Often there are highlighted "C" or "V"-shaped dark marks on the dorsal fin webs. The snout is short and the mouth long. The dorsal fins are short and angular, and it has a slender caudal fin. There are no enlarged rough denticles on the middle of the back.

Found on the continental shelf and upper slope. Partially sexually segregated, the female being more numerous than the male off kwaZulu-Natal, and in equal numbers off Mozambique.

Size Mature: ~9–13 in. ♂, ~8.5–9 in. ♀. Max: 13 in.
Distribution Western Indian Ocean: South Africa (kwaZulu-Natal), southern Mozambique (type specimens caught off Cape Point).
Food Small bony fish, crustaceans, and cephalopods.
Breeding Eggs laid in pairs.
Status Not evaluated. Formerly common, but not caught in research trawls for ~15 years. Entire range heavily fished.

Izak Catshark *Holohalaelurus regani*

This catshark is yellowish to yellow-brown and white below, with scattered tiny black dots beneath the very broad head. The upper surface is covered with dark brown reticulations, bars, and blotches. The Natal subspecies, however, has smaller reticulations and is more like a checkerboard or spotted. The snout is short, and the mouth long. The short dorsal fins are angular and the caudal fin is slender. It has enlarged rough denticles on the middle of the back.

Both subspecies occur on the continental shelf and upper slopes. At least part of the population migrates inshore in the fall. The northeastern subspecies juveniles occur in deeper water than the adults. In the typical subspecies, the juveniles are in shallower water than the adults.

Size Typical subsp.: Mature: 18–27 in. ♂, 15.75–20.5 in. ♀.
NE subsp.: Mature: 20.5–21.5 in. ♂, 15–17 in. ♀. Max: 27 in. TL.
Distribution Southeastern Atlantic, southwestern Indian Ocean. Typical subspecies: Namibia to South Africa. Northeastern subspecies: South Africa and Mozambique.
Food Small bony fish, crustaceans, cephalopods, polychaetes, hydrozoans, occasionally kelp.
Breeding Oviparous, pairs of eggs laid year round.
Status Not evaluated. Discarded bycatch. Typical subspecies population increasing, northeastern subspecies status uncertain.

Filetail Catshark *Parmaturus xaniurus*

A soft, flabby, plain dark catshark, brownish black above, lighter below, with all fins dark and enlarged gill slits. The snout is moderately long and blunt, with large triangular anterior nasal flaps and ridges under the eyes. It has a crest of sawlike denticles along the top of the caudal fin, hence its name. The dorsal fins are similar sized and the second dorsal fin is much smaller than the anal fin, with its insertion well in front of anal fin insertion.

Adults live often on or near the bottom of the outer continental shelf and upper slope; the juveniles, however, live in midwater and in water over 3,300 ft. deep.

These catsharks have been observed from submersibles, feeding on moribund lanternfish in almost anoxic conditions The squalene-filled liver may maintain neutral buoyancy. The enlarged gills enable it to thrive in its low-oxygen habitat.

Size Adult: 14.5–18 in. ♂, 18.5–22 in. ♀ TL.
Distribution Northeastern Pacific: Oregon to Mexico (Gulf of California).
Food Mainly pelagic crustaceans and small bony fish.
Breeding Oviparous, egg cases with "T"-shaped lateral flanges and short tendrils.
Status Data deficient. Relatively common. Discarded from bottom trawls and sablefish traps.

Onefin Catshark *Pentanchus profundicolus*

A unique plain brownish catshark, similar in appearance to the demon catsharks. It is the only species of shark to have five gill slits and one dorsal fin. The abdomen is unusually short, the pectoral and pelvic fins are very close together. The snout is broadly rounded, the mouth is short, as are the gill slits which have incised septa. The nostrils are large and widely spaced. It has long, narrow caudal fins that do not have a crest of denticles. Its anal fin is very long and low.

The two specimens found occured on insular slopes on the bottom in relatively deep water, between 2,210 ft. and 3,510 ft. Hardly anything is known about this species.

Size Adult: 20 in. TL ♂. Max: unknown.
Distribution Northwestern Pacific: Philippines (Tablas Straits and Mindanao Sea, east of Bohol).
Food Not known.
Breeding Not known.
Status Not evaluated. Known from two specimens.

Leopard Catshark *Poroderma pantherinum*

This is a striking, leopardlike catshark with its rosettes of dark spots and lines surrounding lighter centers, which are usually arranged in irregular longitudinal rows. Variations do occur and include numerous small dense spots to very large dark spots and partial longitudinal stripes. The long nasal barbels reach the mouth, which extends behind the front of the eyes. The dorsal fins are set far back, with the first being much larger than the second.

Leopard Catsharks live on or near the bottom of the continental to upper slope, from the surf zone and intertidal area. They are apparently nocturnal.

Size Mature: 21–23 in. ♂, 23–24 in. ♀. Max: 29 in. TL.
Distribution Southeastern Atlantic and western Indian Ocean: apparently endemic to South Africa (both Capes, rarely to kwaZulu-Natal). Records from Mauritius and Madagascar require verification.
Food Small bony fish and invertebrates.
Breeding Oviparous, one egg/oviduct.
Status Not evaluated. Taken by trawlers and anglers. Hardy when kept in aquaria. Large-spotted variant formerly considered a separate species, the Barbeled Catshark.

Narrowtail Catshark
Schroederichthys maculatus

This catshark is extremely slender and has an elongated trunk and tail in juveniles and adults. The juvenile's pattern is six to nine light, inconspicuous brown saddles on a darker tan to gray background. This disappears in adults to three saddles in the interdorsal space and numerous scattered white spots appear, but there are no dark spots. The snout is rounded, with broad, elongated, triangular anterior nasal flaps. Its mouth is wide and deep. The first dorsal begins slightly behind the pelvic fin's insertions.

It lives on shelly or sandy bottoms in deepwater, on tropical outer shelves and upper slopes.

Size Mature: <11 in. TL ♂. Max: 14 in. TL.
Distribution West Atlantic: Central and South America off Honduras, Nicaragua, and Colombia, and between the Honduras Bank and Jamaica.
Food Small bony fish and squid.
Breeding Oviparous, probably lays pairs of eggs, with tendrils on cases.
Status Not evaluated.

Whitesaddled Catshark *Scyliorhinus hesperius*

This is a fairly small and slender catshark. It has a conspicuous dark bar under the eye and seven or eight well defined dark saddles densely covered with large, closely spaced white spots, which sometimes extend to the lighter spaces between saddles. It has no black spots. Their anterior nasal flaps are small and end in front of the mouth with no nasoral grooves. The labial furrows are on the lower jaw only and the second dorsal fin is much smaller than the first.

This is a little known species that lives on the upper continental slope, on or near the bottom.

Size Adult females reach at least 18.5 in. TL.
Distribution West Atlantic (Caribbean): Honduras, Panama, Colombia.
Food Not known.
Breeding Not known.
Status Data deficient. Adult habitat may be untrawlable.

Chain Catshark *Scyliorhinus retifer*

The Chain Catshark has distinctive black chain patterning outlining faint dusky saddles, which is unique to this species and the Reticulated Swellshark (page 136). The Chain Catshark has well developed lower labial furrows and the dorsal fins are set well back.

It lives on the outer continental shelf and upper slope, on or near the bottom, from 240 to 2,475 ft., deeper in the south. It is possibly most common on very rough, rocky untrawlable areas which are suitable for egg laying. It is a sluggish shark, often found resting on the bottom. It may swallow small pebbles, perhaps for ballast. The females wrap egg case tendrils up to 14 in. long around seabed projections, such as corals, by rapid circular swimming.

Size Mature: 15–19.5 in. ♂, 14–20 in. ♀. Max: 23 in. TL. Young reach 10–12 in. in two years in captivity.
Distribution Northwestern Atlantic, Gulf of Mexico, and Caribbean: U.S. (Georges Bank, MA, to Florida and Texas), Mexico (Campeche Gulf), Barbados, area between Jamaica and Honduras, Nicaragua.
Food Squid, bony fish, polychaetes, and crustaceans.
Breeding Oviparous, eggs laid in pairs every 8–15 days in captivity during spring and summer. Eggs hatch after about seven months in captivity, longer in nursery areas.
Status Least concern. Common where it occurs.

Smallspotted Catshark *Scyliorhinus canicula*

A common species in its range. Used to be called the Lesser Spotted Dogfish, which is a misnomer because it is a catshark. It is large, slender, and covered in numerous small dark spots on a light background. There are eight or nine dusky saddles, which may not be distinct. It has greatly expanded anterior nasal flaps that reach the mouth and cover the shallow nasoral grooves. Only the lower jaw has labial furrows. Its second dorsal fin is much smaller than the first.

They occur on sediment from nearshore on continental shelves and upper slopes. The adults are often found in single-sex schools, with the young and hatchlings in shallower water.

Size Mature: Mediterranean; 15 in. ♂, 17 in. ♀. Larger in Atlantic and North Sea. Max: North Sea; 39 in. TL.
Distribution Northeastern Atlantic: Norway and British Isles to Mediterranean, Canary Islands, Azores, to Ivory Coast.
Food Small bottom invertebrates (crustaceans, gastropods, cephalopods, worms) and fish.
Breeding Oviparous, egg cases deposited in pairs year round.
Status Not evaluated. Taken in many fisheries, retained and discarded, but it has a high discard-survival rate and some populations are stable or increasing.

Nursehound *Scyliorhinus stellaris*

A very large and stocky catshark with many large and small black spots and sometimes white spots, over a pale background. Their saddles, if present, are very faint. The large spots may be irregular and occasionally expand into large blotches, which totally cover the body.

It is found on the continental shelf, from just below the surface down to 410 ft., but commonly from 66 to 206 ft., on rocky or seaweed-covered bottoms. They deposit large, thick-walled egg cases with strong tendrils at the corners on algae. The easiest way to tell these two species apart is that in the Nursehound the anterior nasal flaps do not reach the mouth.

Size Egg case: 4–5 in. long. Common to 49 in. Max: 64 in. TL.
Distribution Northeastern Atlantic: southern Scandinavia to Mediterranean, Morocco, Canaries, Mauritania to Senegal. Records farther south to Gulf of Guinea and Congo River mouth may be *Scyliorhinus cervigoni*.
Food Mostly crustaceans, cephalopods, other mollusks, bony fish, and other small sharks.
Breeding Oviparous. Single egg/oviduct laid in spring and summer, may take nine months to hatch.
Status Not evaluated. Limited fisheries interest. Less common than the Smallspotted Catshark.

Finback Catsharks

These are dwarf to small sharks, adults from 5 to 25.5 in., with narrowly rounded heads and rounded or subangular snouts. They have no deep groove in front of the elongated, catlike eyes, which have rudimentary nictitating eyelids. There are no barbels or nasoral grooves and the internarial space is narrow, less than 1.3 times the nostril width. They have long angular arched mouths that reach past the anterior ends of their eyes. Their labial furrows are very short or even absent. The first dorsal fin bases are short and well ahead of the pelvic fin bases, but closer to pelvic fin bases than the pectoral fin bases. They do not have precaudal pits and their caudal fins are without a strong ventral lobe or lateral undulations on their dorsal margin. The body and fin color is usually variegated, but the *Eridacnis* species have plain bodies and striped caudal fins.

Most of them are ovoviviparous, except for the oviparous Graceful Catshark, and feed on small fishes and invertebrates. They are poorly known deepwater sharks of the outer continental and insular shelves and upper slopes, and are usually found on or near the bottom. Most occur in the Indo-west Pacific but some in the tropical northwestern Atlantic.

A recently discovered finback catshark, the Clown or Magnificent Catshark

Cuban Ribbontail Catshark *Eridacnis barbouri*

A very small, slender, light grayish-brown catshark with light edges on the two dorsal fins and faint dark banding on the long, narrow, ribbonlike caudal fin. The anal fin is about two-thirds of the dorsal fin heights. It has nictitating eyelids and a triangular mouth with very short but well developed labial furrows. The anterior nasal flaps are short and do not reach the mouth. They have no nasoral grooves or barbels.

They live on the upper continental and insular slopes, usually on the bottom.

Size Born: >4 in. TL. Mature: ~10.5 in. ♂, 11 in. ♀.
Max: 13 in. TL.
Distribution Northwestern Atlantic: Florida Straits and off northern coast of Cuba.
Food Not known.
Breeding Ovoviviparous, two pups/litter.
Status Not evaluated. Relatively common or formerly common in its limited range.

Harlequin Catshark *Ctenacis fehlmanni*

This catshark has a somewhat stout body and tail, with a unique color pattern of large, reddish-brown, irregular dorsal saddle blotches interspersed with smaller round spots and vertical bars, and spots on the fins. It has nictitating eyelids and a large triangular mouth with very short labial furrows. Their anterior nasal flaps are short and do not reach the mouth.

All specimens found on the outer continental shelf.

Size Max: 18 in. TL (adult ♀).
Distribution Northwestern Indian Ocean: off Somalia.
Food Large mouth, small teeth, and large pharynx with gill rakers suggest a diet of very small invertebrates.
Breeding Possibly ovoviviparous (the very thin-walled large egg case in each uterus of the holotype would probably have been retained until the pair of young hatched).
Status Not evaluated. Known from only a few specimens.

Graceful Catshark *Proscyllium habereri*

As the name suggests, this catshark has a slender body with a rather long tail and a broad caudal fin. It has small to large dark brown spots, sometimes with small white spots and indistinct dusky saddle blotches on the body and fins. The eyes are large with nictitating eyelids. Unlike the previous two finback catsharks, it has large anterior nasal flaps that nearly reach the triangular mouth, which extends past the eyes.

Found on the continental and insular shelves.

Size Adult 17–22 in. ♂, 20–25.5 in. ♀. Max: 25.5 in. TL.
Distribution Western Pacific: Northwestern Java, Vietnam, China, Taiwan, Korea, Ryu-Kyu Islands, southeastern Japan.
Food Bony fish, crustaceans, and cephalopods.
Breeding Oviparous, one egg/uterus.
Status Not evaluated.

False Catsharks & Gollumsharks

These are small to large sharks, adults from 22 in. to 116 in., with narrowly rounded heads and more or less elongated bell-shaped snouts, with a deep groove in front of the elongated, catlike eyes. The eyes have rudimentary nictitating eyelids. They have no barbels or nasoral grooves and the internarial space is relatively large, more than 1.5 times the nostril width. The mouth is long, angular, and arched, reaching past the anterior ends of the eyes. Their labial furrows are short, but always present. The first dorsal fin is more or less elongated, its base is closer to the pectoral fin bases than to the pelvic fin bases. They have no precaudal pits and the caudal fin has a weak ventral lobe or none at all. Their caudal fins have no lateral undulations on their dorsal margins. They are usually plain gray to brown or blackish, however some *Gollum* species do have white spots and fin margins.

As far as it is known, they are all ovoviviparous, with at least two species known to be oophagous, with the fetuses eating infertile eggs. They probably prey on small fishes and invertebrates. These are poorly known deepwater sharks of the outer continental and insular shelves and slopes. They occur on or near the bottom, from 425 ft. to 745 ft. The large False Catshark is wide ranging, but the small species have restricted distributions in the western Indian Ocean and the western Pacific. They are absent from the South Atlantic and eastern Pacific.

False Catshark *Pseudotriakis microdon*

These are unpatterned dark brown to blackish large sharks with a stocky, bulky, soft body and tail. Their large body cavity, soft fins, skin, and musculature indicate they are an inactive and sluggish shark with virtually neutral buoyancy. They have elongated catlike green eyes with nictitating eyelids. The snout is short and bell-shaped when viewed dorsoventrally and wedge-shaped laterally. They have short anterior nasal flaps and a huge angular mouth that extends behind the eyes. The labial furrows are short. Their spiracles are very large and are about as long as their eyes. They have numerous small teeth (more than 200 rows per jaw). The first dorsal fin is long, low, and keel-like, with the second dorsal fin much taller.

They inhabit deepwater seabeds on the continental and insular slopes and occasionally occur on continental shelves and near shallower submarine canyons.

Size Mature: 78–106 in. ♂, 83–116 in. ♀. Max: 116 in. TL.
Distribution Patchy worldwide, except (so far) South Atlantic or eastern Pacific.
Food Photographed feeding on a fish in deepwater.
Breeding Ovoviviparous: two, possibly four pups/litter. Apparently oophagous.
Status Data deficient. Seemingly uncommon or rare wherever it occurs.

Gollumshark *Gollum attenuatus*

This is an unpatterned grayish, small shark with a slender body and tail. It has elongated catlike eyes, with nictitating eyelids. The snout is very long and angular, bell-shaped in dorsoventral view and wedge-shaped laterally. The anterior nasal flaps are short and the angular mouth extends behind the eyes with short labial furrows. Its spiracles are small and it has numerous small teeth, more than 120 rows per jaw. The first dorsal fin is relatively short and subtriangular, the second is as high or slightly higher.

It lives on the outermost continental shelf, upper slope, and adjacent seamounts.

Size Mature: ~27.5 in. (♂ and ♀). Max: 43 in. TL.
Distribution New Zealand, surrounding seamounts and ridges.
Food Not known.
Breeding Ovoviviparous and oophagous, two pups/litter.
Status Least concern. Taken as bycatch, but low fishing effort in range.

Barbeled Catshark *Leptocharias smithii*

A small, slender, light gray-brown shark whose eyes are horizontally oval and with internal nictitating eyelids. Its nostrils have slender barbels. The long arched mouth reaches past the anterior ends of the eyes, the labial furrows are very long, and the teeth are small and cuspidate. Peculiar to this species is that males have greatly enlarged anterior teeth.

It lives near the bottom of continental shelves and is especially common on mud off river mouths. Little is known about its behavior. It is thought that males may use their greatly enlarged front teeth in courtship and copulation.

Size Mature: ~21.5–23.5 in. ♂, ~20–23 in. ♀. Max: 32 in. TL.
Distribution Eastern Atlantic: Mauritania to Angola, possibly to Morocco and Mediterranean.
Food Crustaceans, small bony fish, and skate.
Breeding Viviparous, with unique spherical placenta. Pregnant females occur July–October off Senegal. Seven pups/litter, gestation period at least four months.
Status Near threatened. Taken in many fisheries as utilized bycatch throughout its restricted habitat; status needs further study.

Houndsharks

One of the largest families of sharks with more than 40 species, found worldwide in warm and temperate coastal seas. Most of the species occur in continental and insular waters, from the shoreline and intertidal to the outermost shelf, often close to the bottom. Many are found in sandy, muddy, and rocky inshore habitats, enclosed bays, and near river mouths. There are a few deepwater species that range down continental slopes to great depths, possibly greater than 6,560 ft. Many are endemic with a very restricted distribution.

Small to medium-sized sharks with two medium to large spineless dorsal fins and an anal fin. Their horizontally oval eyes have nictitating eyelids. They have no nasoral grooves, and the anterior nasal flaps are not barbel-like, except for the Whiskery Shark. Their mouths reach past the front of their eyes and have moderate to very long labial furrows. Some species (i.e. *Mustelus*) can be very hard to identify without vertebral counts and many species are undescribed.

They can be very active, swimming almost continuously, others can rest on the bottom, and many swim close to the seabed. Some are most active by day, others at night. Houndsharks are either ovoviviparous or viviparous. They feed mainly on bottom and midwater invertebrates and bony fish; some take largely crustaceans, some mainly fish, and a few primarily cephalopods; none feed on birds and mammals.

Houndsharks are generally fairly common and some are very abundant in coastal waters and fished extensively for their meat, liver oil, and fins (i.e. Tope and smoothhounds). Some of the smaller coastal species reproduce rapidly and can support well managed fisheries. Others have a history of stock collapse where fisheries are unregulated and require much more careful management. Some species are extremely rare. None are harmful to people.

Whiskery Shark *Furgaleus macki*

This is the only houndshark with its anterior nasal flaps forming slender barbels. It is stocky, almost humpbacked in appearance, with obvious ridges below the dorsolateral eyes. Its mouth is very short and arched. Gray above, with variegated dark blotches or saddles that fade with age, and light below.

Whiskery sharks are found on or near the bottom on rocky bottoms, in seagrass meadows, or kelp beds, in shallow temperate seas on the continental shelf. They are active swimmers searching out their favorite prey, octopus.

Size Mature ~43 in. TL. Max: 59 in. TL.
Distribution Australia.
Food Specialist feeder on octopus, also takes squid, bony fish, and lobsters.
Breeding Ovoviviparous, no yolk-sac placenta, 4–29 pups/litter (average 19) every second year.
Status Least concern. Common. Stock depleted by target gillnet fishery to <30% of original size in 1960s–70s. Fishery now well managed, population fairly stable since mid 1980s, and now increasing.

Tope *Galeorhinus galeus*

This is a large, slender, long-nosed houndshark without obvious anterior nasal flaps or subocular ridges. The mouth is large and arched with small bladelike teeth. The second dorsal fin is much smaller than the first and about as large as the anal fin. Tope have extremely long terminal caudal lobes, up to half the length of the dorsal caudal margin. They are grayish above and white below, with black markings on the fins of the young.

Most abundant in cold to warm temperate continental seas, from the surfline and very shallow water to well offshore, but not oceanic, and often near the bottom. This shark is an active, strong, long-distance swimmer and can travel more than 31 miles in a day. It usually occurs in small schools, partly segregated by size and sex, which are seasonally highly migratory in higher latitudes, with migrations of 985 miles recorded. The pregnant females move into shallow bays and estuaries to give birth and then return to their offshore feeding grounds.

The juveniles remain in nursery grounds for up to two years, then join the schools of immatures in other locations. The females mature late, normally after 10 years, and they can possibly live for 60 years.

Size Vary between regions. Mature: ~47–70 in. ♂, 52–73 in. ♀. Max: 69 in. ♂, 77 in. ♀ TL.

Distribution Worldwide in temperate waters.

Food Mainly an opportunistic feeder on bony fish, also invertebrates. Predators include other large sharks and probably marine mammals.

Breeding Ovoviviparous, no yolk-sac placenta, 6–52 pups/litter, increasing with size of mother. Very low biological productivity.

Status Vulnerable. Fished all over the world for meat, liver oil, and fins. Also taken by sport anglers. Many populations are seriously depleted and most fisheries unmanaged. It is critically endangered in the southwestern Atlantic.

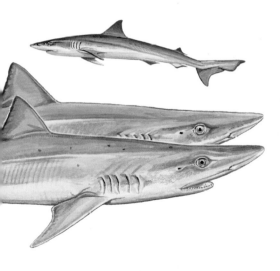

Sailback Houndshark *Gogolia filewoodi*

A small, gray-brown houndshark that is distinguished by its huge triangular first dorsal fin, which is about half the length of the caudal fin. It also has a long preoral snout, just over half again the width of the mouth. The description of this shark is based on only one specimen.

The only known specimen was found at 240 ft. on the continental shelf, probably near the bottom.

Size Mature: ♀ measured 29 in. TL.
Distribution Southern Pacific: one site known, northern New Guinea.
Food Not known.
Breeding Ovoviparous. Pregnant female was carrying two pups.
Status Data deficient. Presumably an uncommon endemic.

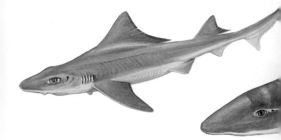

Striped Smoothhound *Mustelus fasciatus*

A distinctive gray houndshark with vertical dark bars on an unspotted body. These bars fade with age and become indistinct. Fairly stocky with a very long head and long, angular, acutely pointed snout with widely spaced nostrils. The eyes are very small. Its teeth are arranged in pavement form and without cusps, the crowns being broadly rounded. The dorsal fins are broadly triangular and unfringed. The caudal peduncle is short. This houndshark closely resembles the Speckled Smoothhound, but has a longer, more angular head.

   Found on temperate continental shelf and uppermost slope, on bottom inshore and offshore.

Size Mature: >24 in. ♂. Max: 61 in. TL.
Distribution Southwestern Atlantic: southern Brazil, Uruguay, northern Argentina.
Food Not known.
Breeding Viviparous, with placenta.
Status Critically endangered. Pregnant females and young taken as bycatch in intensive coastal fisheries.

Japanese Topeshark *Hemitriakis japanica*

This houndshark has fairly low, slitlike eyes with a clearly defined ridge below and small bladelike teeth. The fins are conspicuously white-edged, but are not strongly curved in the adults. The first dorsal fin's origin is over or slightly behind the pectoral fin's free rear tips, except in newborns, and the anal fin is much smaller than the dorsal fins. The snout is moderately long and parabolic, the mouth broadly arched and the anterior nasal flaps short.

It occurs close inshore to more than 330 ft. deep in offshore waters on the temperate to subtropical continental shelf.

Size Mature: ~33.5 in. ♂, 31–39 in. ♀. Max: 43 in. ♂, >47 in. TL ♀.
Distribution Western Pacific: China (including Taiwan), Korea, Japan.
Food Not known.
Breeding Ovoviviparous, no yolk-sac placenta, 8–22 pups/litter, increasing with size of female. In East China Sea, mating occurs June to September (mostly June to August) and pupping in June to August (mainly June).
Status Not evaluated. A commonly utilized fisheries bycatch.

Blacktip Topeshark *Hypogaleus hyugaensis*

This fairly slender, medium-sized houndshark is bronze to gray-brown with a lighter underside. The dorsal and upper caudal fin tips are dusky, particularly in the young. It has a long, broadly pointed snout, large oval eyes and bladelike teeth. The second dorsal fin is smaller than the first but larger than the anal fin. It has a relatively short terminal caudal lobe, which is less than half the dorsal fin's caudal margin.

Dwells near the bottom on tropical and warm-temperate continental shelves and uppermost slope.

Size Mature: ~37–43 in. Max: >51 in. TL.
Distribution Western Indian Ocean: South Africa, Tanzania, Kenya. Northwestern Pacific: Taiwan, Japan. Southwestern Pacific: Australia.
Food Bony fish and cephalopods.
Breeding Viviparous, yolk-sac placenta, 8–11 pups/litter. Pups in December in South African waters and in February off Australia, after estimated 15-month gestation.
Status Near threatened. Patchy distribution and generally low abundance. Bycatch in fisheries.

Bigeye Houndshark *lago omanensis*

A slender, uniform grayish-brown houndshark with a lighter underside. Its dorsal fin margins are sometimes dusky. The gill slits are large; the longest slit may be nearly as long as the length of the very large eyes. The teeth are small and bladelike. It has small dorsal fins with the origin of the first set far forward over the pectoral fin's bases.

Lives on or near the bottom of the continental shelf and slope. Often found in warm, oxygen-poor conditions. Little is known about its behavior. The enlarged gills may permit survival in warm, low-oxygen, and probably hypersaline waters.

Size Mature: <12 in. ♂, <16 in. ♀. Max: 23 in. ♀ TL. Male much smaller than female.
Distribution Indian Ocean: Red Sea, Gulf of Oman, Pakistan, southwestern India, possibly Bay of Bengal and Burma (Myanmar). Sharks similar to this species in the Bay of Bengal may be a separate distinct species.
Food Bony fish and cephalopods.
Breeding Viviparous, yolk-sac placenta, 2–10 pups/litter.
Status Not evaluated.

Starry Smoothhound *Mustelus asterias*

This is the only European smoothhound with many small white spots on gray or gray-brown sides and back, with no dark spots or bars. It has large nostrils that are set closer together than similar species in the region. It has a "pavement" of flat teeth. The dorsal fins are unfringed and the pectoral and pelvic fins are fairly small.

Found on or near sand and gravel bottoms, on continental and insular shelves. In captivity they swim actively. It is thought they may migrate inshore in the summer. They are a popular fish for anglers.

Size Mature: 31–33 in. ♂, ~33 in. ♀. Max: 55 in. TL.
Distribution Northeastern Atlantic: North Sea to Canaries, Mediterranean, and Mauritania.
Food Specialist feeder on crustaceans.
Breeding Ovoviviparous, no yolk-sac placenta, 7–15 pups/litter, increasing with maternal size, born inshore in summer after about one year gestation. Mature at two to three years.
Status Least concern. Fisheries bycatch with low market value.

Grey Smoothhound *Mustelus californicus*

This is a locally common unpatterned, uniformly gray smoothhound. The head is short and narrow with widely spaced nostrils. Its eyes are fairly large and the mouth is short with a "pavement" of flat teeth and equal-sized, upper and lower, labial furrows. The dorsal fins are triangular and the first is closer to the pelvic fins than pectorals. It has a poorly developed ventral caudal lobe.

This is a schooling species, occuring on the bottom of continental shelves and shallow muddy bays, inshore and offshore warm-temperate to tropical waters. A summer visitor to north-central California waters and resident farther south.

Size Mature: 22-25.5 in. ♂, ~27.5 ♀. Max: 45.5 ♂, 49 in. ♀ TL.
Distribution Northeastern Pacific: northern California to Gulf of California.
Food Mostly crabs.
Breeding Viviparous, two–five pups/litter.
Status Not evaluated. Common where it occurs. Important in fisheries in south.

Dusky Smoothhound *Mustelus canis*

A large, slender, usually unspotted gray smoothhound, with a short head and snout. "Pavement" of low, flat teeth. The nostrils are widely spaced, but the large eyes are closely spaced and the upper labial furrows are longer than the lower. It has a deeply notched caudal fin. Newborn young have dusky-tipped dorsal and caudal fins.

Occurs in two habitats. The continental shelf subspecies prefers mud and sand at less than 60 ft., but can occur down to 650 ft. and rarely on the uppermost slopes to 1,180 ft. The island subspecies prefers rough rocky bottoms on the outer shelves and upper slopes, and may occur in midwater off Cuba. These are very active sharks, constantly patroling for food that can be located even when hidden. The northern population migrates inshore and north in the summer, south and offshore in the winter. They are not territorial in captivity, but larger animals are dominant.

Size Mature: ~32 in. ♂, 35 in. ♀. Max: 59 in. TL.
Distribution Northwestern Atlantic: Canada to Argentina, in several widely separated discrete populations.
Food Not known.
Breeding Viviparous, with yolk-sac placenta, bearing 4–20 pups/litter. Matures in one to two years.
Status Near threatened. Abundant where it occurs. Largest females fished heavily by long line and gill net. Declines reported. Kept in public aquaria.

Smoothhound *Mustelus mustelus*

A large, fairly slender, usually unspotted gray to gray-brown smoothhound, with a short head and snout. The nostrils are widely spaced and the large eyes are close-set. Its upper labial furrows are slightly longer than the lower, and the low-crowned teeth have weak cusps. The ventral caudal lobe is more developed than the previous species and semifalcate. Occasionally has sporadic dark spots.

Smoothhounds are voracious and active predators of the continental shelves and upper slopes. They prefer swimming near the bottom, but are sometimes found in midwater.

Size Mature: 27.5–29 in. ♂, ~31 in. ♀. Max: at least 43 in. ♂, 64.5 in. TL ♀.
Distribution Temperate eastern Atlantic: Britain to Mediterranean, Morocco, Canaries, possibly Azores, Madeira. Angola to South Africa, including Indian Ocean coast.
Food Primarily a crustacean feeder, also cephalopods and bony fish.
Breeding Viviparous, yolk-sac placenta, 4–15 pups/litter after 10–11 months gestation.
Status Least concern. Common to abundant. Very important in fisheries in European, Mediterranean, and West African waters. Taken in bottom trawls, fixed nets, and line gear. Used fresh, frozen, dried-salted, and smoked for food; liver for oil, and for fishmeal. Also taken by sport anglers. Kept in aquaria.

Flapnose Houndshark
Scylliogaleus quecketti

A blunt short-snouted houndshark with large, fused nasal flaps expanded to cover the mouth, hence its common name. Nasoral grooves are present and the teeth are small, blunt and pebblelike. The second dorsal fin is as large as the first and much larger than the anal fin. It is grayish above and cream below. Newborns have white rear edges on the dorsal, anal, and caudal fins.

Occurs on the inshore continental shelf, at the surfline to close offshore.

Size Mature: <27.5 in. ♂, <31 in. ♀.
Max: 40 in. TL.
Distribution Western Indian Ocean: South Africa.
Food Primarily crustaceans (including lobsters), also squid.
Breeding Bears litters of two–four (usually two or three) pups after a gestation of nine–ten months.
Status Vulnerable. Restricted where distribution is heavily fished and population is small.

Spotted Gully Shark *Triakis megalopterus*

A gray-bronze houndshark, usually with many black spots, and white below. The young have no or few spots and some adults are also plain. Spotted Gully Sharks have a broad blunt snout, a large mouth, and pointed small teeth. The fins are large and broad and there is a high interdorsal ridge present. The caudal peduncle is short and heavy.

They live in the shallow inshore to the surfline, preferring sandy shores and rocks, and crevices in shallow bays. They school in summer with many pregnant females often present. An active patroller of the bottom in captivity, they are sometimes found in midwater, but rarely in the open.

Size Mature: 51–55 in. ♂, 55–59 in. ♀.
Max: poss. 67 in. TL.
Distribution Southern Angola to South Africa.
Food Crabs, bony fish, small sharks.
Breeding Ovoviviparous, no yolk-sac placenta, 6–10 pups/litter.
Status Near threatened. Locally common but range is heavily fished. Caught by sport anglers and commercial fishers, but of low commercial value. Hardy in captivity.

Leopard Shark *Triakis semifasciata*

An unmistakable shark with its unique pattern of black saddle marks and spots on a pale tan to grayish background, fading to whitish below. The marks become light-centered in adults.

Found in cool to warm temperate inshore and offshore waters, on the continental shelf, and are commonest on or near the bottom. An active, strong-swimming shark, forming large nomadic schools, sometimes with the Brown and Gray Smoothhounds and also the Piked Dogfish. Most Leopard Sharks have a small range, but some travel up to 95 miles. Sometimes rests on sand among rocks.

Size Mature: 27.5–47 ♂, 43–51 in. ♀. Max: 59 in. ♂, 71 in. ♀ TL.
Distribution Northeastern Pacific, Oregon to Gulf of California.
Food Opportunistic feeder of bottom animals, including burrowing invertebrates. Diet varies with size and season.
Breeding Ovoviviparous, no yolksac placenta, 4–29 pups/litter. Slow growing and late to mature.
Status IUCN Red List: Lower Risk (conservation dependent). Common to abundant where it occurs. Valuable flesh, intensive commercial and sport fishing led to declines, but U.S. population now well managed. Status in Mexico unknown. Very hardy; readily adapts to captivity when young.

Weasel Sharks

Small to moderate-sized sharks with horizontal oval eyes and nicitating eyelids. They have small spiracles, long labial furrows, precaudal pits, and large second dorsal fins. The caudal fins have a strong ventral lobe and a wavy dorsal edge.

They are live bearing. Some are specialist feeders on cephalopods, others have a very varied diet.

Atlantic Weasel Shark *Paragaleus pectoralis*

An unmistakable slender shark with striking longitudinal yellow bands on light gray or bronze background and white below. It has a moderately long snout, large oval eyes, and a short small mouth. All the fins are plain.

Occurs on the tropical shelf, from the surfline to 330 ft.
Size Mature: ~31.5 in. ♂, 29.5–35.5 in. ♀. Max: 54 in. TL.
Distribution Eastern Atlantic: Cape Verde Islands and Mauritania to Angola, possibly north to Morocco.
Food Specialist feeder on cephalopods (squid and octopi), also small fish.
Breeding Bears one–four pups/litter in May to June in Senegal.
Status Not evaluated.
Common where it occurs.

Snaggletooth Shark *Hemipristis elongatus*

This is a slender, light gray- or bronze-colored shark with no prominent markings. The snout is broadly rounded and long. Its common name describes the large, curved saw-edged upper teeth, which are in contrast to the hooked lower teeth that protrude from the mouth. The gill slits are long and most of the fins are strongly concave curved. The tip of the second dorsal and the terminal lobe of the caudal fins sometimes have a dusky blotch, which is more prominent in the juveniles.

Found on the continental and insular shelves, from just below the surface at 3 ft. to 435 ft.

Size Mature: ~43–47 in. Max: 90.5–94 in. TL.
Distribution Indo-west Pacific: South Africa to northern Australia, Philippines, and China.
Food Cephalopods and fish.
Breeding 2–11 pups/litter, increasing with female size. Pregnancy seven–eight months, possibly breeds in alternate years.
Status Vulnerable. Important, intensively fished commercial species with declining stocks reported.

Hooktooth Shark *Chaenogaleus macrostoma*

A small, slender, light gray or bronze shark, often without prominent markings, but sometimes with black tips to the second dorsal fin and terminal lobe of the caudal fin. So named because of its extremely long, hooked, smooth-edged lower teeth that protrude from the very long mouth. It has a fairly long, angular snout, large lateral eyes with nictitating eyelids, small spiracles, and gill slits at least twice as long as the eye length. The second dorsal fin is about two-thirds the size of the first. The pectoral fins and to some extent the caudal fin, are pointed.

Found on the continental and insular shelves, down to 195 ft. Thought to be relatively common because of the frequency of catches by fisheries in the area.

Size Mature: 27–38 in. ♂. Max: ~39 in. TL.
Distribution Indo-west Pacific: Gulf to Indonesia and China.
Food Probably small fish, octopus, and squid.
Breeding Poorly known; four pups/litter.
Status Not evaluated. Commonly caught in fisheries.

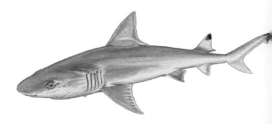

Sicklefin Weasel Shark
Hemigaleus microstoma

A similar-looking small, slender, light gray or bronze shark, as the Hooktooth. However, the dorsal fins have light margins and tips and there are sometimes white spots on the sides. The snout is fairly long and rounded, the gill slits are short and the mouth very short and arched. Its pelvic and dorsal fins, as well as the ventral caudal lobe, are strongly falcate and pointed at the tips, hence its common name. The second dorsal fin is about two-thirds the size of the first and directly opposite the equal-sized anal fin.

A seemingly common shark on or near the bottom of the continental shelf.

Size Mature: ~23.5 in. Max: 36–37 in. TL.
Distribution Tropical Indo-west Pacific: India to Philippines and China.
Food Probably a specialist feeder on cephalopods.
Breeding Not known.
Status Least concern. Heavily fished, but apparently reproduces very rapidly, with fast population growth rates.

Requiem Sharks

Requiem Sharks are found in all warm and temperate seas and are one of the largest and most important shark families, with many common and wide-ranging species. They are often the dominant sharks in tropical waters on the continental shelves and offshore. A few species enter temperate or deep waters. This family also includes the only freshwater shark species.

They are mostly medium to large sharks, although there are exceptions, and have long arched mouths with bladelike teeth and no nasoral grooves or barbels. The eyes are usually round with internal nictitating eyelids and usually no spiracles.

They are active, strong swimmers. Some species are "ram-ventilators" needing to swim continually to oxygenate their gills, others can rest on the bottom. Many are more active at night, or dawn and dusk, than by day. Some are solitary or socialize in small groups, others are social schooling species. Some give specialized threat or defensive displays and may also interact aggressively when they encounter each other. There is a clear hierarchical dominance between certain species, for example, Oceanic Whitetip Sharks are dominant over Silky Sharks of the same size, which in turn can dominate Grey Reef Sharks. They are major predators, taking a wide range of prey. Some larger species opportunistically eat carrion and refuse, but none are specialist scavengers.

They are very important in tropical shark fisheries. Several species are potentially harmful, having bitten humans and boats, but are also important for dive ecotourism.

**Juvenile
Tiger Shark**

Tiger Shark *Galeocerdo cuvier*

A huge striped shark, whose stripes are bold in the young but fade with age. It has a broad, bluntly rounded snout, very long upper labial furrows, and a big mouth and spiracles.

Tiger Sharks are found on or near the continental and insular shelves, from the surface and intertidal to possibly 460 ft. They can travel long distances between islands. Adults appear to be nocturnal, moving inshore at night to very shallow water, and deeper areas by day. Usually solitary but may aggregate when feeding. They are fast growing, maturing at four to six years and live at least 12 years.

Size Mature: 89–114 in. ♂, 98–138 in. ♀.
Max: ~216.5 in. TL.
Distribution Worldwide, temperate and tropical seas.
Food Sometimes called "a garbage can with fins": eats bony fish, elasmobranchs, sea turtles, sea snakes, marine iguanas, seabirds, marine mammals, carrion, and refuse.
Breeding The only ovoviviparous carcharhinid.
Status Near threatened. Common or formerly common large shark but caught regularly in target and nontarget fisheries (fins are high value). Some declines reported. Potentially harmful; responsible for fatal attacks on people, but often unaggressive when encountered underwater. Valuable for dive tourism.

Silky Shark *Carcharhinus falciformis*

This is a large, slim, dark gray to gray-brown, or nearly blackish shark. They have a fairly long, flat, rounded snout, small jaws, and large eyes. The second dorsal fin is low with a greatly elongated inner margin and rear tip, and long narrow pectoral fins. They have a narrow interdorsal ridge, but no caudal keels.

Silky Sharks are oceanic and epipelagic, from the surface to at least 1,640 ft. Longline catches are much more abundant offshore near land, than in the open ocean. They are active, swift, bold, inquisitive, and sometimes aggressive sharks—divers have reported seeing sharks hunch their backs as a threat. Often found with tuna schools in the east Pacific.

Size Mature: ~74–85 in. ♂, 84–90.5 in. ♀. Max: ~130 in. TL.
Distribution Worldwide in tropical seas.
Food Primarily eats fish, also cephalopods and pelagic crabs.
Breeding Viviparous, yolk-sac placenta, 2–14 pups/litter.
Status Under review. One of the three most common oceanic sharks, huge bycatch in oceanic fisheries. Landed for meat and fins. Susceptible to overfishing; serious declines reported in some areas. Potentially harmful to people, but rarely encountered except at offshore reefs near deep water. Important for ecotourism in the Red Sea.

Blue Shark *Prionace glauca*

A slim, graceful shark with a dark blue back, bright blue flanks, and a sharp demarcation to the white underside. They have a long conical snout, large eyes, long narrow scythe-shaped pectoral fins, and no interdorsal ridge.

These sharks are oceanic and pelagic, usually off the edge of the continental shelf, from the surface to 1,150 ft.. They are highly migratory. They cruise slowly at the surface, the tips of their dorsal and caudal fins out of the water. They may form large aggregations, where they are still sufficiently abundant, to feed on shoals of prey or carrion.

Size Mature: 72–111 in. ♂, ~86 in. ♀. Max: 150 in. TL.
Distribution They are worldwide in temperate and tropical oceanic waters and may be the most wide ranging of sharks.
Food Feed on smallish prey, usually squid and pelagic fish.
Breeding Viviparous, yolk-sac placenta, 4–135 pups/litter.
Status Near threatened. The most heavily fished shark in the world, many millions taken annually, mainly as bycatch. Meat is low value but the large valuable fins are kept and enter the international shark-fin trade (often after carcasses are discarded at sea). Recent reports of about 60–80% decline in catch rates and reductions in frequency of sightings. Potentially harmful, they are responsible for a few fatal bite incidents on people, but are often timid.

Bull Shark *Carcharhinus leucas*

A large, thick-headed grayish shark, with a very short, broad, bluntly rounded snout and small eyes. Their first dorsal fin is triangular with a short rear tip. They have no interdorsal ridge, but do have an inconspicuous caudal keel.

They are usually found close inshore, from just under the surface to at least 500 ft., in lagoons, bays, river mouths, 62 miles upstream in warm rivers, and even in freshwater lakes. Often they cruise slowly near the bottom, but they are agile and quick when chasing and attacking prey.

Size Mature: 62–89 in. ♂, 71–90.5 in. ♀. Max: ~134 in. TL.
Distribution Worldwide, tropical, and subtropical seas.
Food Takes a very broad range of food, from invertebrates and fish, to sea turtles, whale offal, and terrestrial mammals.
Breeding Viviparous, yolk-sac placenta, 1–13 pups/litter.
Status IUCN Red List: Near threatened. Bycatch throughout its range; populations depleted rapidly if targeted. Nearshore and estuarine habitat vulnerable to human impacts. Because of its large size, indiscriminate appetite, and abundance in coastal areas where human activities occur, this is potentially the most dangerous of tropical sharks; well known for several fatal and nonfatal bites on people. Very popular for dive ecotourism. Popular sport angling trophy.

Oceanic Whitetip Shark
Carcharhinus longimanus

This is a large, stocky, gray or brownish shark, with huge rounded first dorsal fin and long paddlelike pectoral fins with obvious white-mottled tips. The snout is bluntly rounded and the eyes are small. It has an interdorsal ridge and inconspicuous caudal keels.

It is oceanic to epipelagic, occasionally coastal, usually found far offshore in warm open seas. It is slow moving but active by day and at night, cruising slowly at or near the surface. They are very inquisitive, aggressive, and persistent, but rarely encountered.

Size Mature: 69–78 in. ♂, ~71–79 in. ♀.
Max: ~138–155.5 in. TL.
Distribution Worldwide, tropical to warm temperate waters.
Food Mainly oceanic bony fish and cephalopods, but also sea birds, and turtles to carrion and refuse.
Breeding Viviparous, yolk-sac placenta, 1–15 pups/litter.
Status Near threatened. Originally widespread and common, but has a low reproductive capacity and huge numbers have been taken in bycatch and directed fisheries, with some massive population decreases. Has been responsible for biting swimmers and boats.

Bignose Shark *Carcharhinus altimus*

A cylindrical, heavy-bodied shark, which is grayish, sometimes bronze above and white below. It has no conspicuous markings but for the dusky fin tips, except on the pelvic fins, and faint white flank markings. The snout, as their common name suggests, is large, long, and broad, with long nasal flaps. It has a prominent high interdorsal ridge, and large straight pectoral and dorsal fins. The caudal fin is comparatively long.

Bignose Sharks occur offshore on deep continental and insular shelf edges and uppermost slopes. The young are found in shallow waters. Sometimes appear on the surface.

Size Mature: 85 in. ♂, 89 in. ♀.
Max: ~118 in. TL.
Distribution Probably worldwide in tropical and warm seas, but records incomplete.
Food Bony fish, other sharks, stingrays, cuttlefish.
Breeding Viviparous, 3–15 pups/litter.
Status Data deficient. Bycatch of deep pelagic longlines and occasionally bottom trawls.

Bronze Whaler *Carcharhinus brachyurus*

Also called the Copper Shark, it is olive-gray to bronze above, and white below. Most fins have an inconspicuous darker edge and blackish tips. It has a large, bluntly pointed, broad snout and usually no interdorsal ridge. The pectoral fins are long and the dorsal fins are small with short rear tips.

Found close inshore to at least 330 ft. deep offshore. These are active sharks, seasonally migrating in at least part of their range. Large numbers follow winter sardine runs off South Africa. The nursery grounds are in inshore bays and coasts.

Size Mature: 79–90 in. ♂, <94 in. ♀. Max: 115 in. TL.
Distribution Most warm temperate waters in Indo-Pacific, Atlantic, and Mediterranean.
Food Bony fish, elasmobranchs, and cephalopods.
Breeding Viviparous, yolk-sac placenta.
Status Near threatened. Exceptionally slow growth rate, inshore habitat vulnerable to damage, and easy to capture. Caught for food and by sport anglers. Potentially harmful to swimmers and divers and sometimes aggressive during encounters with divers.

Silvertip Shark *Carcharhinus albimarginatus*

A striking dark gray, sometimes bronze-tinged shark, with brilliant white tips and trailing edges on all fins. The pectoral fins have narrow tips.

Found on the continental shelf, on offshore islands, coral reefs, and offshore banks; also inside lagoons, near dropoffs and offshore. Young found in shallower water closer inshore than the adults. Often follow boats and are more aggressive than and dominant over the Galapagos and the Blacktip Sharks.

Size Mature: 63–71 in. ♂, 63–78 in. ♀. Max: ~118 in. TL.
Distribution Tropical Indo-Pacific, wide but patchy distribution. Unconfirmed in western Atlantic.
Food A variety of midwater and bottom fish and octopi.
Breeding Viviparous, yolk-sac placenta, 1–11 pups/litter.
Status Data deficient. Large and slow growing. Even remote populations are highly vulnerable to target fisheries for meat or fins. Large, bold, and potentially harmful, caution is advised when encountering it underwater.

Gray Reef Shark *Carcharhinus amblyrhynchos*

A gray shark with an obvious broad, black posterior margin to the entire caudal fin, and blackish tips to other fins.

Found on continental and insular shelves and adjacent oceanic waters, coastal-pelagic and inshore. Common on coral reefs, often in deeper areas near dropoffs and shallow lagoons adjacent to strong currents.

An active, strong-swimming social species, aggregating by day in or near reef passes or lagoons. Often cruises near the bottom. Even more active at night, when groups disperse. Inquisitive, with an intimidating threat display.

Size Mature: 43–57 in. ♂, 47–54 in. ♀.
Max: poss. 92–100 in. TL.
Distribution Indo-west to central Pacific.
Food Mostly bottom feeds on small bony reef fish, also cephalopods (squid and octopi) and crustaceans.
Breeding Viviparous, yolk-sac placenta, one–six pups/litter.
Status Near threatened. One of the most abundant Indo-Pacific reef sharks. Formerly common, now under threat. More valuable protected for dive tourism than for fisheries, but can be aggressive (particularly when spearfishing is occurring) and may bite if cornered, harassed, or when food stimuli are present.

Blacktip Reef Shark
Carcharhinus melanopterus

This is an abundant medium-sized brownish-gray shark, with brilliant black fin tips, highlighted by white. They have short bluntly rounded snouts, horizontally oval eyes, narrow-cusped teeth, and no interdorsal ridge. The largish second dorsal fin has a short rear tip.

It is found in very shallow water on coral reefs and reef flats, also near reef dropoffs and in brackish water. They are strong, active swimmers, often with the dorsal fin above the surface in very shallow water. Occurs either alone or in small groups (it is not strongly schooling). Undergoes tidal migrations, often within a limited territorial range.

Size Mature: 36–39 in. ♂, 38–44 in. ♀. Max: <70 in. TL.
Distribution West Pacific, Indian Ocean, and eastern Mediterranean (a migrant through the Suez Canal).
Food Small fish and invertebrates.
Breeding Viviparous, yolksac placenta, two–four pups/litter.
Status Near threatened. One of the most common Indo-Pacific reef sharks. Regularly caught by inshore fisheries and likely depleted. Probably adversely affected by reef destruction. Important for aquarium display and for dive tourism, very occasionally bites people swimming or wading on reefs but more wary when encountering divers.

Whitetip Reef Shark *Triaenodon obesus*

This small, slender grayish-brown shark has brilliant, very conspicuous white tips on the first dorsal and upper caudal fin. It sometimes has scattered dark spots on sides.

These reefsharks occur on continental shelves and island terraces. Usually on or near the bottom in crevices or caves, in coral reefs, and in coral lagoons in shallow clear water. They are often seen resting on the bottom, in caves and under ledges in coral, and on sand by day. More active during slack tide and at night. They are social but not territorial; sharing home ranges without conflict. Readily attracted to bait, but rarely aggressive.

Size Mature: 41–41.5 in. ♂, 41.5–43+ in. ♀.
Max: ~79 in. TL.
Distribution Indo-Pacific Ocean.
Food Specialize in capturing bottom prey, located by scent and sound, sometimes in packs.
Breeding Viviparous, one–five pups/litter.
Status Near threatened. Often very common, but restricted depth range, habitat, and small litter size suggest that increased fishing pressure may be a threat. Popular for dive tourism, kept in captivity.

Spinner Shark *Carcharhinus brevipinna*

This is a gray shark with most fins (apart from those of the young) having obvious black tips. It has a slender, long, narrow pointed snout, small circular eyes, and prominent labial furrows, longer than any other *Carcharhinus*. The pectoral and first dorsal fins are small.

Spinner sharks are coastal to pelagic on continental and insular shelves, common close inshore. They are active, schooling sharks, which get their name from their vertical feeding runs through fish schools that end with a spinning leap out of the water. Highly migratory in Gulf of Mexico and possibly elsewhere. There is some segregation by age and sex

Size Mature: 62.5–80 in. ♂, 67–79 in. ♀. Max: 109 in. TL.
Distribution Warm temperate and tropical Atlantic, Mediterranean, and Indo-west Pacific.
Food Primarily a fish-eater; also stingrays and cephalopods.
Breeding Viviparous, yolk-sac placenta, 3–15 pups/litter.
Status Near threatened. Common, but inshore distribution vulnerable to fishing pressure and habitat change. Valuable meat and fins, important in multispecies fisheries. Has bitten swimmers and may be of concern to spear fishermen.

Blacktip Shark *Carcharhinus limbatus*

A fairly large, stout, gray to gray-brown shark, with fin tips usually black on the pectorals, the second dorsal, and the ventral caudal lobe and sometimes on the pelvic fins, but rarely on the anal fins. There are usually black edges on the first dorsal apex and dorsal caudal lobe.

Found on the continental and insular shelves, usually close inshore, occasionally offshore but rarely more than 98 ft. These sharks are very active, fast swimmers, often in large surface schools. They may leap out of the water and rotate up to three times at the end of a feeding run on small schooling fish, but do so less often than Spinner Sharks.

Size Mature: 53–71 in. ♂, 47–75 in. ♀. Max: 100 in. TL.
Distribution Widespread tropical and subtropical seas.
Food Mainly fish, also cephalopods and crustaceans.
Breeding Viviparous, yolk-sac placenta, one–ten pups/litter.
Status Near threatened. Inshore distribution is heavily fished and susceptible to habitat degradation. An important commercial and sport angling species. Very few serious bites on people reported –not harmful unless stimulated by food. Important for dive tourism.

Finetooth Shark *Carcharhinus isodon*

A small, dark bluish-gray shark, with a white underside and an inconspicuous white band on the flank. It has no prominent fin markings. The snout is moderately long and pointed, the eyes are fairly large, and the gill slits are very long. The teeth are erect and either smooth or irregularly serrated, hence its common name. It has no interdorsal ridge, the pectoral and first dorsal fins are small, but the second dorsal fin is moderately large.

These sharks occur in the warm temperate to tropical waters of the inner continental shelf. They are very active and form large schools or aggregations when they migrate seasonally as water temperature changes.

Size Mature: ~52 in. ♂, 49–53 in. ♀.
Max: poss. 74–79 in. TL.
Distribution West Atlantic: United States to Brazil.
Food Small fish, also shrimp.
Breeding Viviparous, yolk-sac placenta, two–six pups/litter.
Status Not evaluated. Locally common, bycatch throughout range, also targeted on migration. Inshore habitat vulnerable to degradation.

Night Shark *Carcharhinus signatus*

This is a slim gray-brown shark. Its underside is white and there are no conspicuous fin markings. It has a long, pointed snout, small jaws, small pectoral fins, and large eyes. The front of the first dorsal fin is over the pectoral fins and both dorsal fins are low with elongated rear tips. It does have an interdorsal ridge.

This is a deepwater coastal and semioceanic shark found on or along the outer continental and insular shelves and off upper slopes. Like the Finetooth, Night Sharks are an active schooling shark, but they migrate vertically, every night, into shallower water. They are named for their tendency only to be seen at night. There could be seasonal geographic migrations similar to the Finetooth.

Size Mature: ~75–79 in. Max: 110 in. TL.
Distribution Tropical Atlantic: U.S. to Argentina and western Africa.
Food Small active bony fish, squid, and shrimp.
Breeding Viviparous, yolk-sac placenta, 4–18 pups/litter.
Status Vulnerable. Formerly very common in Caribbean fisheries, now apparently rare. Harmless to people.

Sandbar Shark *Carcharhinus plumbeus*

This is a stout gray-brown or bronze shark, often with dusky tips and posterior edges to the fins. It has a very large erect first dorsal fin and an interdorsal ridge.

Sandbar Sharks are common in bays, harbors, and at river mouths, but also offshore in adjacent deep water and on oceanic banks, usually near the bottom. Some stocks migrate seasonally, often in large schools, as the water temperatures change. The adults are segregated from the juveniles and the sexes are usually separate except when mating in the spring and summer. One of the slowest growing and latest maturing of coastal sharks.

Size Mature: ~55–71 in.
Max: ~94.5, possibly 118 in. TL.
Distribution Worldwide, tropical and warm temperate waters.
Food Mainly small bottom fish.
Breeding Viviparous, yolk-sac placenta, 1–14 pups/litter.
Status Near threatened. Common and widespread in subtropical and warm temperate waters. Severely overfished in the western North Atlantic where meat and fins are extremely valuable. Hardy and spectacular in public aquaria.

Lemon Shark *Negaprion brevirostris*

A big, stocky, short-nosed, pale yellow-brown shark. The second dorsal is about as large as the first.

An inshore and coastal species, it ranges from the surface and intertidal to at least 300 ft. It is usually found around coral keys, mangrove fringes, enclosed sounds or bays, and river mouths, because it is adapted to low-oxygen shallow-water environments. It may travel short distances upriver. Lemon sharks are most active at dawn and dusk and rest on the bottom when inactive. They may migrate seasonally, sometimes swimming at or near the surface in open ocean.

Size Mature: ~88 in. ♂, ~94 in. ♀. Max: 134 in. TL.
Distribution Tropical western Atlantic, northeastern Atlantic (western Africa), eastern Pacific (Mexico to Ecuador).
Food Mainly fish, also crustaceans and mollusks.
Breeding Viviparous, yolk-sac placenta, 4–17 pups/litter.
Status Near threatened. Some coastal nursery grounds are subject to habitat deterioration. Evidence of some population depletion by unmanaged fisheries in eastern Pacific and western Atlantic. Valuable for dive tourism. Potentially harmful, can be aggressive when provoked.

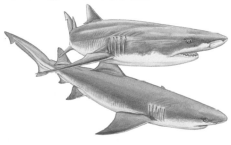

Dusky Shark *Carcharhinus obscurus*

This is a large gray to bronze shark with most fin tips dusky, but not boldly, marked. Its underside is white, with an inconspicuous white band on the flanks. It has a broadly rounded snout, curved, moderately-sized pectoral fins, large falcate first dorsal fin, and low interdorsal ridge.

Dusky sharks occur on the continental and insular shelves, from the shoreline to the adjacent oceanic waters. Often seen offshore following ships. They are strongly migratory, moving with changing temperatures between temperate and subtropical areas. The young form large feeding schools or aggregations.

Size Mature: ~110 in. ♂, 101–118 in. ♀. Max: 142–157.5 in. TL.
Distribution Possibly worldwide in tropical and warm temperate waters.
Food Bony fish are primary prey, followed by elasmobranchs and crustaceans, with other species also taken.
Breeding Viviparous, yolk-sac placenta, 3–14 pups/litter.
Status Near threatened. One of the vertebrates most vulnerable to exploitation because it reproduces so slowly. Difficult to manage or protect because it is taken in mixed species fisheries, and has a high mortality rate when taken as bycatch. Very occasionally bites people. Young are kept in aquaria.

Caribbean Reef Shark *Carcharhinus perezi*

A large, dark gray or gray-brown reef shark. The undersides of the paired fins, and the anal and ventral caudal lobe are dusky but not prominently marked. The short snout is bluntly rounded, the pectoral fins are large and narrow, and there is an interdorsal ridge present.

This is the commonest Caribbean coral reef shark, living on the outer reefs to at least 98 ft. Usually prefers a hard seabed, but occurs on mud off river deltas in Brazil. These reef sharks can lie motionless on the bottom, pumping water over their gills with their pharynx. They can be closely approached while lying "sleeping" in caves or in the open.

Size Mature: ~60–66 in. Max: 116 in. TL.
Distribution Western Atlantic and Caribbean: North Carolina to Brazil.
Food Bony fish.
Breeding Viviparous, yolk-sac placenta, three–six pups/litter.
Status Near threatened. Common and very heavily fished for human consumption, hides, oil, and fins but far more valuable for dive tourism. Often encountered by divers without incident; rarely bites people.
Kept in a few large aquaria for public viewing, and has given birth in captivity.

Ganges Shark *Glyphis gangeticus*

This is one of only a few sharks that apparently live permanently in freshwater. It is a large stocky shark, gray above and white below, without conspicuous markings. The short snout is broadly rounded and the eyes are tiny. It has no interdorsal ridge but does have a longitudinal upper precaudal pit. The anal fin has a deeply notched posterior margin.

It lives in large freshwater rivers, possibly estuaries and inshore coastal waters. A little-known species.

Size Mature: ~70 in. ♂. Max: possibly at least 80 in. TL and probably larger.

Distribution Indo-west Pacific: Ganges-Hooghly river system, India. Nominal records over a wide range in the Indo-west Pacific were often based on the Bull Shark or other species and cannot be confirmed.

Food Not known.

Breeding Probably viviparous.

Status Critically endangered. Originally known from three 19th-century museum specimens. Recent records need confirmation; a set of jaws was recently collected from a specimen of what seemed to be this species in the mouth of the Hooghly River. Habitat heavily fished and degraded. Man-eating reputation may be caused by the Bull Shark.

Atlantic Sharpnose Shark
Rhizoprionodon terraenovae

A medium-sized gray to gray-brown shark with small light spots in larger specimens. It has a white underside, light to white margined pectoral fins, and dusky-tipped dorsal fins.

These sharks prefer shallow coastal water in enclosed bays, sounds, harbors, and marine to brackish estuaries. They occur from the intertidal zone to about 110 ft. deep, but usually shallower than 35 ft. They are often close to the surf zone off sandy beaches. Seasonal migration in the Gulf of Mexico, from offshore in the winter to inshore in the spring.

Size Mature: 25.5–31 in. ♂, 33–35 in. ♀.
Max: at least 43 in. TL.
Distribution Northwestern Atlantic.
Food Mainly small bony fish.
Breeding Viviparous, yolk-sac placenta, one–seven pups/litter.
Status Least concern. Abundant and able to sustain fairly intensive fishing pressure.

Daggernose Shark
Isogomphodon oxyrhynchus

An unmistakable, unpatterned gray or yellow-gray shark. The snout is extremely long, flat, and pointed, and from above it looks like a dagger blade. It has tiny circular eyes, large paddle-shaped pectoral fins, and more than 45 rows of small spikelike teeth in both jaws.

Daggernose Sharks live in turbid water in estuaries, mangroves, river mouths, and over shallow banks. These sharks move inshore in the dry season and offshore in the rainy season, suggesting they are intolerant of reduced salinities. Females tend to occur in deeper waters than the males. Their long snout and small eyes may be adaptations for life in turbid water.

Size Mature: 35.5–43 in. ♂, 41–44 in. ♀.
Max: 60 in., possibly 79–96 in. TL.
Distribution Tropical western Atlantic, northern South America.
Food Small schooling fish.
Breeding Viviparous, yolk-sac placenta, three–eight pups/litter. Possible two-year birth cycle.
Status Critically endangered. Bycatch in fisheries. Population declining steeply.

Broadfin Shark *Lamiopsis temmincki*

A small, rather stocky, light gray to tan shark. It is light below but has no prominent markings. The moderately long snout is nearly as long as the mouth is wide. The upper and lower teeth are differentiated; the upper teeth are serrated with broad triangular cusps and the lower are smooth with hooked, narrow cusps. It has small round eyes, and the fifth gill is half the height of the first. The large second dorsal fin is nearly the same size as the first. There is a longitudinal upper precaudal pit and the pectoral fins are broad and triangular.

Little is known about this inshore continental shelf shark.

Size Mature: ~45 in. ♂, >51 in. ♀. Max: 66 in. TL.
Distribution Scattered in Indian Ocean and west Pacific. Common (formerly?) near Mumbai (Bombay), western India.
Food Not known.
Breeding Viviparous, four–eight pups/litter (usually eight), born before the monsoon.
Status Not evaluated. Rare. Taken in fisheries, trends unknown.

Sliteye Shark *Loxodon macrorhinus*

This small shark is very slim, gray to brownish, with a white underside. All the fins have an inconspicuous, light, rear edge and the first dorsal and caudal fins have black margins. The snout is long and narrow. Its big eyes have an obvious posterior notch from which it gets its common name. The mouth has short labial furrows and small, smooth-edged oblique-cusped teeth. It has a small, low, second dorsal fin with a very large free posterior margin and an interdorsal ridge can be either absent or rudimentary.

Sliteye Sharks are found on continental and insular shelves in shallow, clear water. Its behavior is unreported.

Size Mature: 24–26 in. ♂, 31 in. ♀. Max: 36 in. TL.
Distribution Indo-west Pacific.
Food Small bony fish, shrimp, and cuttlefish.
Breeding Viviparous, yolk-sac placenta, two–four pups/litter.
Status Least concern. Commonly caught in fisheries. Presumed fast growing and able to sustain reasonable fishing pressure.

Whitenose Shark *Nasolamia velox*

A distinct, slender, gray-brown to light brown shark with a very long, conical snout, large round eyes, and very large close-set nostrils, separated by a space only slightly greater than the nostril width. Its common name comes from the white patch outlining a prominent black spot on the upper snout tip.

Occurs on the continental shelf, inshore and offshore. Little is known about the behavior of this shark.

Size Mature: >42 in. ♂. Max: at least 59 in. TL.
Distribution Tropical eastern Pacific, Central America: Baja California, Mexico, to Peru.
Food Small bony fish and crabs.
Breeding Viviparous, yolk-sac placenta, five pups/litter.
Status Not evaluated. Taken with long lines for food and fishmeal. Formerly uncommon to rare where it occurs.

Milk Shark *Rhizoprionodon acutus*

A small bronze to grayish shark, which is white below, with most fin tips slightly pale. The juvenile's dorsal and upper caudal fin tips are dark, which may still occur in some adults. It has a long narrow snout, big eyes, oblique narrowly triangular smooth-edged teeth, and a small, low, second dorsal fin behind a larger anal fin. It is the only requiem shark in its range with long upper and lower labial furrows.

Milk Sharks live on the continental shelf, from midwater to near the bottom, just below the surface down to 650 ft. They are often off sandy beaches and sometimes in estuaries with not very low salinity. They are eaten by larger sharks, so because of the decline in large shark numbers, this shark has increased. They are called Milk Sharks because it was thought their flesh, if eaten, would help milk production in mothers.

Size Mature: about 27–28 in. ♂, about 27.5–32 in. ♀.
Max: 70 in. TL (usually <43 in.).
Distribution Eastern Atlantic, Indo-west Pacific.
Food Mainly bony fish.
Breeding Viviparous, yolk-sac placenta, one–eight pups/litter.
Status Least concern. Heavily fished, but productive, common, and widespread.

Spadenose Shark *Scoliodon laticaudus*

Another shark easily identified by the shape of its snout. It is a small, stocky bronze-gray shark with no conspicuous markings, but the snout is unmistakable. It is very long, flattened, and spadelike when viewed from above, hence its name. It has small eyes, small, smooth-edged, bladelike teeth, short, broad triangular pectoral fins, and a second dorsal fin much smaller than the first, originating well behind the origin of the larger anal fin. There is no interdorsal ridge.

These sharks are found close inshore, often in rocky areas and the lower reaches of large tropical rivers. They occur in large schools, which makes them easy targets for fisheries.

Size Mature: 9–14 in. ♂, 13–14 in. ♀.
Max: ~29 in. TL.
Distribution Indo-west Pacific.
Food Small pelagic schooling and bottom-living bony fish, also shrimp and cuttlefish.
Breeding Viviparous, unusual columnar placenta and numerous long appendiculae on umbilical cord.
Status Near threatened. Abundant but very heavily fished.

Hammerhead Sharks

Members of this family of sharks are unmistakable with their hammer-shaped heads. These function as a submarinelike bow plane to improve their maneuverability and increase sensory capacity by enhancing their stereoscopic vision and ability to triangulate sources of scent and electromagnetic signals.

They are all live bearers (viviparous), with yolksac placenta. Because many are large predators they feed on bony fish, smaller sharks, rays, cephalopods, and invertebrates, but not on marine mammals or other large vertebrates.

They are found worldwide in tropical and warm temperate seas, on or adjacent to continental and insular shelves and seamounts. Some species form large spectacular schools. Unfortunately, target and bycatch fisheries have depleted many populations; their fins are highly valuable and hammerheads die very quickly when hooked or entangled, so live release of bycatch is unusual. Some large species, like the Great Hammerhead and possibly the Scalloped and Smooth Hammerheads have occasionally bitten divers and swimmers, but most are shy and very difficult to approach.

Winghead Shark *Eusphyra blochii*

The most bizarrely shaped hammerhead with its immense wing shaped, narrow, bladed head. The width between the eyes is about half the total length of the shark. The first dorsal fin's origin is over the pectoral fin's bases, further forward than any other hammerhead. The upper precaudal pit is longitudinal, not crescent-shaped.

Winghead Sharks live in shallow water, on continental and insular shelves. Pregnant females have been reported to fight each other.

Size Mature: ~39 in. TL. Max: 73 in. TL.
Distribution Indo-west Pacific: northern Indian Ocean to Australia and China.
Food Not known.
Breeding Six (usually)–nine pups/litter.
Status Near threatened. Heavily fished in much of range.

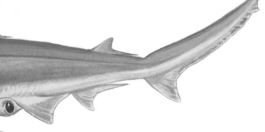

Winghead Shark

Scalloped Hammerhead *Sphyrna lewini*

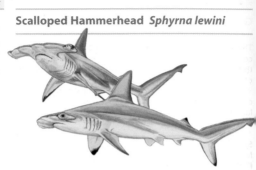

A large shark with a broadly arched, narrow-bladed head with a central notch and two smaller, lateral indentations. It has dusky or black-tipped pectoral fins and a dark blotch on the lower caudal fin lobe.

These sharks occur over the continental and insular shelves and adjacent deep water, from the surface to more than 900 ft. When in coastal waters they often enter bays and estuaries. They are seasonally migratory, schooling, coastal to pelagic semioceanic sharks and have been seen feeding socially.

Size Mature: 55–65 in. ♂, ~83 in. ♀. Max: 145.5–165 in. TL.
Distribution Worldwide, in warm temperate and tropical seas.
Food Bony fish, sharks, rays, and invertebrates.
Breeding 13–31 pups/litter.
Status Near threatened. Common and widespread, but extremely heavily fished in most areas.

Great Hammerhead *Sphyrna mokarran*

This is a very large hammerhead with a single notch at the center of its head. The first dorsal fin is very high and curved, the second dorsal and pelvic fins are also high, with deeply concave rear margins, all fins are unmarked.

A coastal pelagic and semioceanic shark, found over continental shelves and island terraces, also in passes and lagoons of coral atolls and on coral reefs. Nomadic and seasonally migratory.

Size Mature: 92–106 in. ♂, 98–118 in. ♀.
Max: 216.5–240 in. TL.
Distribution Worldwide, tropical seas.
Food Varied prey; apparently prefers stingrays and other batoids, groupers, and sea catfishes.
Breeding 6–42 pups/litter.
Status Data deficient. Not abundant. May occasionally bite people.

GLOSSARY

Abdominal ridges or keels: paired longitudinal dermal ridges that extend from the bases of the pectoral fins to the pelvic fin bases.

Aggregating: to gather into a group.

Amphitemperate: a species that occurs in both the northern and southern hemispheres, but not in the tropics.

Anoxic: without oxygen.

Anterior nasal flap: a flap on the front edges of the nostrils that serves to partially divide the nostril into incurrent and excurrent openings.

Aplacental vivipary: live-bearing in which the young do not have a yolk-sac placenta.

Barbels: long, conical, paired dermal lobes on the snouts of sharks, which may serve to locate prey.

Bathypelagic zone: part of the oceans beyond the continental and insular shelves, from about 3,300 ft. to more than 13,125 ft. and above the middle and lower continental rises and the abyssal plain; the sunless zone. Some oceanic sharks may transit the epipelagic, mesopelagic, and bathypelagic zones to the bottom while migrating vertically.

Benthic or Demersal: referring to organisms that are bottom-dwelling.

Boreal: adjective of, or relating to the north or north wind.

Carcharhinoid: a ground shark, member of the order Carcharhiniformes.

Cartilaginous fish: members of the class Chondrichthyes.

Caudal crest: a prominent sawlike row of enlarged pointed denticles along the dorsal caudal margin, and sometimes along the ventral caudal margin of the caudal fin.

Caudal keels: a keel on each side of the caudal peduncle that may extend onto the base of the caudal fin, and forward as a body keel to the side of the trunk.

Cephalopod(a): a class of marine mollusks with prehensile tentacles and large eyes. Included in this group are cuttlefish, squid, and octopus.

Cetacea: an order of marine mammals with modified forelimbs, no visible hind limbs, and a horizontal tail fin, comprised of whales, dolphins, and porpoises.

Chondrichthyes: a major taxonomic group of aquatic, gill-breathing, jawed, finned vertebrates with primarily cartilaginous skeletons, one to seven external gill openings, oral teeth in transverse rows in their jaws, and mostly small, toothlike scales or dermal denticles. Can also be termed sharklike fish or simply sharks.

Circumnarial fold: a raised semicircular lateral flap of skin around the incurrent aperture of a nostril, defined by a circumnarial groove.

Circumnarial groove: a shallow groove defining the lateral bases of the circumnarial folds.

Claspers: paired copulatory organs present on the pelvic fins of male

cartilaginous fishes, for internal fertilization of eggs.

Cloaca: the chamber at the rear of the body cavity of elasmobranchs through which body wastes and reproductive products including sperm, eggs, and young pass, to be expelled through a common opening or vent.

Continental shelf: the gently sloping, shelflike part of the seabed adjacent to the coast, extending to a depth of about 650 ft. The shelves have the greatest diversity of cartilaginous fishes.

Continental slope: the often steep, slopelike part of the seabed extending from the edge of the continental shelf to a depth of about 6,560 ft. The upper and middle part of the slope has the highest diversity of deepwater benthic sharks.

Dermal denticle or Placoid scale: a small toothlike scale found in cartilaginous fishes, usually small and often close-set to one another and covering the body.

Dermal lobes: narrow or broad-based, simple or branched projections of skin along the horizontal head rim and on the chin.

Dorsal: upward, in the vertical direction of the back.

Dorsal fin spine: a large to minute, hard spine on the front edge of one or usually both dorsal fins, which may be lost entirely or buried in the fin bases.

Dynamite fishing: an illegal and highly destructive activity in which explosions occur under the water. Fish and other marine species in the vicinity are killed by the shock waves from the blast, and are then skimmed off the surface or collected from the bottom by divers. Also known as blast fishing.

Endemic: a species or higher taxonomic group of organisms that is only found in a given area.

Epipelagic zone: an area of the ocean beyond the continental and insular shelves, from the surface to the limits of where most sunlight penetrates, about 650 ft. Also known as the sunlit sea or "blue water."

Extirpation: utterly destroy.

Eye notch: a sharp anterior or posterior indentation in the eyelid that cleanly divides the upper and lower eyelids.

Eyespots or Ocelli: large eyelike pigment spots found on the dorsal surface of the pectoral fins or bodies of some sharks, possibly serving to frighten potential enemies.

Falcate: sickle-shaped.

Gill raker denticles: in the Basking Shark, elongated denticles with hairlike cusps arranged in rows on the internal gill openings, which filter out planktonic organisms.

Interdorsal ridge: a ridge of skin on the midback of sharks, in a line between the first and second dorsal fins particularly important in identifying gray sharks.

Internarial: between the nostrils.

Labial folds: lobes of skin at the lateral angles of the mouth, usually with labial cartilages inside them, separated from the sides of the jaws by pockets of skin (labial grooves or furrows).

Labial furrows or labial grooves: grooves around the mouth angles on the outer surface of the jaws of many cartilaginous fishes, isolating the labial folds.

Lateral: outward, in the transverse direction toward the periphery of the body.

Lateral line: a sensory canal system of pressure-sensitive cells that runs along the side of the body, often branching at the head. Detects water movements, disturbances, and vibrations.

Lateral trunk denticle: a dermal denticle from the dorsolateral surface of the back below the first dorsal fin base.

Littoral zone: part of the ocean over the continental and insular shelves, from the intertidal to 650 ft.

Luminescent/bioluminescent: the production and emission of light, as a result of a chemical reaction (usually thermal radiation). During this reaction, the chemical energy is converted into light energy. It is often used by deepwater species as a means of attracting prey. For example, the Cookiecutter shark is thought to use a bioluminescent patch on its underbelly to appear as a small fish to other larger, predatory fish such as tuna and mackerel. When these fish approach and try to consume the "small fish," they are bitten by the shark.

Membrane: a soft, fibrous tissue that covers, lines, or connects plant and animal organs and cells.

Mesopelagic zone: part of the ocean beyond the continental and insular shelves, from about 650 ft. to 3,300 ft., the twilight zone where little light penetrates.

Mesozoic Era: the Mesozoic Era, which began 250 million years ago, starts with the emergence of the first dinosaurs and mammals, and an abundance of reptiles. The Mesozoic Era lasted about 185 million years an ended with the major extinction of dinosaurs and about 50% of marine invertebrates, probably caused by an asteroid impact or by massive volcanic activity. Horseshoe crabs survived.

Nasal aperture: a hole in the surface of each nasal capsule through which the nostril directs water into and out of the nasal organ.

Nasal flap: one of a set of dermal flaps associated with the nostrils, and serving to direct water into and out of them, including the anterior, posterior, and mesonarial flaps.

Nasoral grooves: grooves on the ventral surface of the snout between the excurrent apertures and the mouth. The nasoral grooves are covered by expanded anterior nasal flaps that reach the mouth, and form water channels that allow the respiratory current to pull water into and out of the nostrils and into the mouth. This allows the shark to actively irrigate its nasal cavities while sitting still or when slowly moving.

nictitating lower eyelid: a movable lower eyelid that has special posterior eyelid muscles that lift it and, in some species, completely close the eye opening.

nictitating upper eyelid: a movable upper eyelid that has anterior eyelid muscles that pull it down and close the eye opening.

oceanic: referring to organisms inhabiting the part of the ocean beyond the continental and insular shelves, over the continental slopes, ocean floor, sea mounts, and abyssal trenches.

oophagy: egg-eating, a mode of live-bearing reproduction employing uterine cannibalism; early fetuses deplete their yolksacs early and subsist by eating nutritive eggs produced by the mother.

Ovivipary/Oviparity: a mode of reproduction in which female sharks deposit eggs, enclosed in oblong or conical egg cases, on the bottom and which hatch producing young sharks that are miniatures of the adults

ovovivipary: generally equivalent to yolksac vivipary, live-bearing in which the young are nourished primarily by the yolk in the yolksac, which is gradually depleted and the yolksac reabsorbed until the young are ready to be born.

papillae: small projections of tissue at the base of a hair, tooth, or feather.

pavement form (teeth): teeth that are usually flattened and joined together to form a "pavement" for crushing prey.

pelagic: referring to organisms that are

free-swimming, not bottom-dwelling.

Permian period: the last period of the Paleozoic era, between the Carboniferous and Triassic periods, which lasted for 60,000,000 years.

Pheromone: a chemical substance secreted by some animals, which affects the behavior or physiology of other animals of the same species.

Photophores: conspicuously pigmented small spots on the bodies of most lantern sharks and some kitefin sharks. These are tiny round organs that are covered with a conspicuous dark pigment (melanin) and produce light by a low-temperature chemical reaction.

Placental vivipary: live-bearing in which the young develop a yolk-sac placenta.

Posterior nasal flaps: low flaps or ridges arising on the posterior edges of the excurrent apertures of the nostrils.

Precaudal fins: all fins in front of the caudal fin.

Predorsal ridge: a low narrow ridge of skin on the midline of the back anterior to the first dorsal fin base.

Preoral: situated or located at the front of the mouth.

Reticulated: patterned, often in a netlike design.

Rise: the transitional and less steep bottom zone from the lower slope to the abyss or ocean floor. Few sharks are known from the rise, and those mostly from the upper rise.

Rostrum: the cartilaginous anterior-most structure that supports the prenasal snout including lateral line canals and masses of ampullae. It is absent in a few nonbatoid sharks and in many batoids.

Saddle: darker dorsal marking that is shaped like a saddle and extends downward on either side of the shark but does not meet on the ventral surface.

Seamount: a large, isolated elevation in the open ocean, characteristically of conical form, that rises at least 3,300 ft. from the ocean floor; often a productive area for deepwater fisheries.

Secondary caudal keels: low horizontal dermal keels on the ventral base of the caudal fin.

Secondary lower eyelid: the eyelid below or lateral to the nictitating lower eyelid, separated from it by a groove or pocket.

Spiracle: a small to large opening between the eye and first gill opening of most sharks and rays, representing the modified gill opening between the jaws and hyoid (tongue) arch. Lost in chimaeras and some sharks.

Squalene: a long-chain oily hydrocarbon present in the liver oil of deepwater cartilaginous fishes. It is highly valued for industrial and medicinal use.

Squatinoid caudal fin: hypocercal caudal fins that resemble inverted caudal fins on ordinary sharks. Unique among angel sharks.

Stereoscopic vision: three-dimensional vision.

Subcaudal keel: in a few dogfish sharks a single longitudinal dermal keel on the underside of the caudal peduncle.

Submersibles: a submarine that is designed and equipped to carry out work in deep water, below the levels at which divers can go.

Subterminal mouth or ventral mouth: mouth located on the underside of the head, behind the snout.

Symphisial teeth: larger oral teeth in one row on either side of the symphisis, distal to medials or alternates where present. Symphisials are broader than medials and usually have asymmetrical roots.

Symphisis: the midline of the upper and lower jaws, where the paired jaw cartilages articulate with each other.

Taxonomy: scientific classification system, i.e. the White Shark: Kingdom (Animal), Phylum (Chordata), Class (Chondrichthyes), Order (Elasmobranchii), Family (Lamnidae), Genus (Carcharodon), Species (Carcharias).

Temperate: two circumglobal bands of moderate ocean temperatures usually ranging between 50° and 72°F at the surface, but highly variable due to currents and upwelling: includes the north temperate zone between the Tropic of Cancer to the Arctic Circle and the south temperate zone between the Tropic of Capricorn to the Antarctic Circle.

Terminal mouth: mouth located at the very front of the animal.

Thorn: enlarged, flat conical denticle with sharp, erect crown and a flattened base.

Tropical: circumglobal band of warm coastal and oceanic water, usually above 72°F at the surface (but varying because of currents and upwelling), between the Tropic of Cancer and the Tropic of Capricorn, including the Equator.

Unpaired fins: the dorsal, anal, and caudal fins.

Upper eyelid: the dorsal half of the eyelid, separated by a deep pocket from the eyeball. The upper eyelid fuses with the eyeball.

Uterine cannibalism or Cannibal vivipary: a mode of reproduction in which fetuses deplete their yolksacs early and subsist by eating nutritive eggs produced by the mother (see oophagy) or first eat smaller siblings and then nutritive eggs.

Vent: the opening of the cloaca on the ventral surface of the body between the inner margins and at the level of the pelvic fin insertions.

Ventral: downward, in the vertical direction of the abdomen. See dorsal.

Vivipary: used in two ways in recent literature, as being equivalent to placental vivipary only, or for all forms of live-bearing or aplacental vivipary.

Yolksac placenta: an organ in the uterus of some ground sharks, formed from the embryonic yolksac of the embryo and maternal uterine lining, through which maternal nutriment is passed to the embryo. It is analogous to the placenta of live-bearing mammals.

Yolksac vivipary: live-bearing in which the young are nourished primarily by the yolk in the yolksacs, which is gradually depleted and the yolksacs resorbed until the young are ready to be born.

FURTHER READING

This book is based on *A Field Guide to the Sharks of the World* by Leonard Compagno, Marc Dando, and Sarah Fowler, published by Collins.

The Shark Trust website **www.sharktrust.org** is an excellent source of information and involvement in anything having to do with sharks.

INDEX